Just

Past

Labor

Day

Just

Past

Labor

Day

Kirk Robertson

selected & new poems, 1969–1995

FOREWORD BY

WILLIAM KITTREDGE

University of Nevada Press: Reno, Las Vegas

Western Literature Series

University of Nevada Press, Reno, Nevada 89557 USA
Copyright © 1975, 1976, 1977, 1978, 1979, 1980, 1981,
1984, 1987, 1989, 1995, 1996 by Kirk Robertson
Foreword copyright © 1996 by University of Nevada Press
All rights reserved
Manufactured in the United States of America
Text and cover design by Carrie Nelson House

Library of Congress Cataloging-in-Publication Data

Robertson, Kirk.
    Just past Labor Day : selected and new poems, 1969–
1995 / Kirk Robertson ; foreword by William Kittredge.
        p.   cm. — (Western literature series)
    ISBN 8-87417-284-5 (pbk. : alk. paper)
    I. Title. II. Series.
PS3568.02494J87   1996   96-30695
811'.54—dc20   CIP

The paper used in this book meets the requirements of
American National Standard for Information Sciences—
Permanence of Paper for Printed Library Materials, ANSI
Z39.48-1984. Binding materials were selected for strength
and durability.

Publication of this book was supported by a grant from the
John Ben Snow Memorial Trust. The author would also
like to thank the Sierra Arts Foundation of Reno, Nevada,
for receipt of a grant that enabled him to complete work
on the poems in the final section of the book.

First Printing

05 04 03 02 01 00 99 98 97 96   5 4 3 2 1

for Valería

*To the extent that life seems a process in which
everything is taken away, minimal landscapes are
places where we live out with greater than usual
awareness our search for an exception, for what is not
taken away.* —ROBERT ADAMS

*Saudade, a largely untranslatable term. One definition:
when the absence of someone or something—history,
land, a promise—becomes the biggest presence in
one's life, and a state of being.* —KATHERINE VAZ

*A powdery blackness drifts slowly over my lateness . . .
I lower the lights, lie down on my bed,
And, rolled into the shadows, I see you—*

—ARTHUR RIMBAUD

Contents

Foreword: Notions of Desire   xix
Author's Note   xxiv

Drinking Beer at 22 Below

Wheat Field with Crows, 1890   2
Halloween   3
Blues for a Brontosaurus   4
Small Ritual for Kerouac   5
The Clorox Kid   6
Love Poems   8
Election Night   9
5:30 News   10
Arlee, Montana   11
Owl   12
The Mighty Hunter   13
A Discussion Concerning Lodging   15
Sunday Service at Short Bear's House   16
A Letter to Boston   17
Top Pieces for the Axis Nave   18
A Hole in One   19
Gone in February   20
Easter   21
Snowing and in the Dark   23
A Quiet Man   25
Fahrenheit 451 at 22 Below   29

Shooting at Shadows, Killing Crows

Naming   32
Sundance   34
Captive   35

Jealousy   36

How the Treaty Was Signed   37

What Caused Pimples on People's Heads   38

How the Missionaries Came   39

Measles   40

Eclipse   41

Winter   42

Found Frozen   43

Berdache   44

Heyoka   45

Grief   47

Death   48

Under the Weight of the Sky

Crossroads   54

5:22 A.M.   56

Dead Dog   57

Titanic   58

Thanx for the Drinks Ladies   59

Birthday   62

It's Like Putting on Your Hat While Reaching Out
   for Your Ears   64

The View   65

Larry Moon   66

A Stitch in Time   67

Omen   68

A Reply   69

Last Dance   70

Olympics   71

Ketchup in Ketchum   72

Lovelock to Twin Falls   74

Twin Falls to St. Ignatius   75

Postcard to My Unborn Son   76

Finish High School   77

Gladioli   79

October and Not Much Relief in Sight   81

Incompetent Psychedelic Rotogravure   82

Petroglyphs   83

Montauk Cafe   84

My Father   86

Ice Lines   88

Making Reservations   89

0 and 2   90

The Letter   91

Vietnam   92

Origins, Initiations

Birth   96

Fire   98

Salt   99

Snakes   101

Marriage   102

Assholes   103

Babble   105

Wind   107

Scratch Shot   108

How to Join the Little Fire Fraternity   109

How to Join the Ant Fraternity   110

How to Join the Rattlesnake Fraternity   111

How to Join the Spiral Shell Fraternity   112

How to Join the Eagle Down Fraternity   113

How to Join the Fraternity That Does Not Fast
    from Animal Food   114
How to Join the Hunters' Fraternity   115
How to Join the Cactus Fraternity   116
How to Join the Galaxy Fraternity   117
How to Join the Sword Swallowers Fraternity   118
How to Join the Struck by Lightning Fraternity   119

Reasons and Methods

Smoke   122
Almost Like a Breeze   123
The Bone Game   124
Proverb   125
Charm   126
Advice   127
Hunt   128
Relations   129
Cultural Anthropology   130
Wohaws   131
Teddy Blue Abbot's Recipe   132
Saturday Night, St. Ignatius, Montana   133
What She Did with the Silverware Given to Her by a
    U.S. Congressman   134
Why There Is No Longer a Perpetual Fire Kept in the
    Kiva of Any Pueblo   135
Of Course There Are Many Different Versions of This
    Story, But . . .   136
Desire   137
Powers   138
Mole and the Sky   139
False Spring   140
Spell   141

I-80 Headed West

Powwow   144
Running Low   146
Movin' On   147
Morningland   149
Note to a Painter   150
Nevada   151
Pecan Pies   152
Goin' to the Post Office with My Son   153
Visitor   154
Spiral   155
Dry Spell   156
A Dark Night   157
Monday Night, Lovelock   158
Without Apparent Cause   159
Drumstick for Cody   160
Badlands   161
Adjusting to the Desert   162
I-80 Headed West   164

Piracy

Carpinteria   166
South Laguna   167
Snapshots   168
Rounding Third   169
Listening to Hank Williams   171
For Now   172
Fractions   173
Things to Do at Jane's Cabin   175
Piracy   176

Hindsight

The Photograph   178
On the Dresser   179
Mason Lake   180
Something No One Catches   181
Exactly Eight Degrees   182
When It Will Happen   183
Edges   184
Rheumatoid Variants   186
Hindsight   187

West Nevada Waltz

Mustard Colored Rain   190
The Misfits   191
Looking at Maps   193
Finding Stillwater   195
Mirage Factor   196
Ten Gallon Clouds   198
Reflections in a Desert Wind   199
Distance   201
Fallon   202
Seeing the Light   203
West Nevada Waltz   204

Painting

Coffee   208
Moments   209
The Color of Water   210
How It Is   211

Waiting for the Call   213

Water   214

Tahoe   215

All Day Long   216

Punctuation   217

Gray   218

One Deep Breath   219

A Body of Work   220

Delivering the Show   221

Approaching Valmy   222

Battle Mountain   223

Tonopah   224

November 2nd   225

Gossip   226

Getting Across   227

Thirty-Seven   228

Painting   229

Driving to Vegas

Waiting   232

Driving   233

Four or Five Beers, Dorsey's Bar, Gabbs, Nevada   234

Outside Ely in the Rain   235

Not Quite Dark   236

Sifting   237

It's Not As If Everything Came from New York   238

Schwitters   239

Seurat   240

Neon   241

Pollock   242

Rothko   243

Hopper 244

Arts Administration 245

Twilight in San Juan 246

RNO–LAX 247

Fog at the Borders of the Palms 248

Drawing to an Inside Straight 249

Driving to Vegas 250

Red Web

The Opening 252

Fishin' in the Dark 253

Artists' Statements 257

Personal Values, 1952 258

4:37 A.M. 259

Driving to Montana with V. 260

Out Here 261

Howling 262

Looking 263

Poetics 264

At Workman's 265

Driving God & the Grieving Widow 266

Metaphor 267

Exquisite 268

Candle 269

Dust 270

Fado for a Sultry Afternoon with the Blinds
    Partly Pulled 271

Red Web 272

Desert Saudade

Music   274

Sierra Wind   278

Rimbaud Stops at the Liquor Store in Mojave   279

Talkin' Cow-Calf Pairs at the Coney Island Bar   280

January   281

Traffic   282

Dilemma   283

Thinking About You, Reading Creeley   284

The Ole Mind-Body Split Healed   285

Again and Again   286

Gardening   287

The Perennial's Lament   288

Independence Day   289

Forty-Six   290

The Mizpah Sonnet   291

Red Mountain   292

Desert Saudade   293

Just Past Labor Day

Rodeo's in Town   296

Heart's Correlative   297

Local Knowledge   298

Erotic   299

Fulcrum   300

Nevada Weather   301

Scenes from the French Revolution   302

Amor Fati   303

Night Music   304

Morna   305

Lure   306

Cellaring   307
Poetry Readings, Dim Bulbs & Bad Renditions of
    Chamber Music   308
Just Past Labor Day   309

Acknowledgments   310

Foreword: Notions of Desire

The American West is beginning to discover its next genera-
tion of voices. Kirk Robertson, I have to think, when it all
shakes down, is sure to be one of the writers we listen to with
gratitude. He helps us make sense of our own selves, what we
want, and helps us get started down the road toward defining
what we maybe *ought* to want.

He reminds us that the prime virtue, the one that drives the
rest of the motors in any society, is in the long run taking emo-
tional care of one another and ourselves (however rough-handed
and awkwardly), as in "January":

> *Honey, I'm sorry*
> *would you* please
> *just get back*
> *in the truck*

The West is a young country with wandering in its genes.
Our ancestors were people who wouldn't stay home. My blood-
line left England three hundred and fifty years ago, for New
England, then Michigan, and finally the outback West. As peo-
ple say in eastern Oregon, on the deserts where my forebears
found they were sort of stranded, "the grass over the mountain
may not be greener, but maybe it ain't mowed."

Plus, the view might be glorious. In "Driving to Montana
with V.," Kirk talks about western towns like Gillette and
Goldfield and Havre, and the people who live there, and why

> All of them
> trying to remember
> over five or six beers
> in the center of a hazy valley floor

> What they felt like
> the first time they saw
> those mountain peaks
> break a windy aluminum colored sky

Kirk comes from an Air Force family. He was born in Los
Angeles in 1946, but as what he calls a service brat he bounced

around Arizona, Texas, and New Mexico until returning to Los Angeles for college. He's got a literature degree from Cal State-Long Beach, where he taught before leaving Southern California for good in 1971. He says it just got too weird.

Which is no doubt sort of true, but it also sounds like he comes from the breeding stock that runs in so many families in the West, people who get nervous and restless for no good reason beyond an urge to know what's down the line. In the early 1970s Kirk hit several popular western searching-for-yourself venues—Humboldt County, the Olympic Peninsula, St. Ignatius up at the foot of the ever-glorious stony peaks of the Mission Mountains on the Flathead Reservation in Montana.

After a while people given to this searching tell themselves that they can savor the sadness of finding themselves at the end of some road (real or metaphoric) so long as there's maybe a treasure of unexplored possibilities over the next hill. Once in a while things go perfectly.

She came back to the Mozart Club with him.
That's when the music really began.

They say heartbreak isn't usually life-threatening, but boredom can be.

You watch the tumbleweeds let go
roll with the rippling metal sound
mobile homes make on such a day
and for a while you're moving along
fairly well but any sudden intrusion
or marshaling of the facts
even small ones stretched thin
taut as wire between fenceposts
hangs you up stops you are stuck

Eventually most of us settle. Kirk has lived east of Reno in Fallon, Nevada, since 1976, and says his recent work is often an attempt "to use 'local knowledge' to articulate what a place might mean."

Fallon, he says is "not the kind of place that anyone sets

out to head to, unless of course you're in the Navy—we're the largest 'warfare training center' in the world here, but something spoke to me the first time I drove into the Lahontan Valley and I really can't imagine living anywhere else . . . this is, really, home."

Over the years Kirk has published eighteen chapbooks/ books of poems with various small presses. He says he is "like so many poets who began writing in 60s/70s, a product of the mimeo/offset little magazine world." Kirk has worked as program coordinator for the Nevada State Council on the Arts and the Squaw Valley Community of Writers and is presently employed by the Churchill Arts Council.

After those wandering beginnings Kirk has been in Nevada long enough to be identified as one of their first-string writers. In 1994 he was voted into the Nevada Writer's Hall of Fame. William L. Fox, former director of the Nevada State Council on the Arts, says, "Kirk Robertson's work follows the tradition of William Carlos Williams and Robert Creeley, the stresses of American life and language inextricably linked in a spare, unforgiving cadence."

Kirk's poems talk to us through the off-hand but extremely articulate and ironic lingo of country people who've had to spend maybe more than enough time alone, rehearsing and getting ready to speak their minds with considerable stutter-step eloquence combined with a deep regard for the hard actualities of human existence (call it a primal willingness to cut through the bullshit while never forgetting that elegance helps hold back the night).

As William L. Fox says, Kirk makes it look easy. "It looks inevitable, the making of a life out of his art, so naturally do the poems seem to arrive from the circumstances. But it's not easy, and hardly inevitable."

Useful art lets us in on the processes of a soul speaking to itself as in Shakespearean soliloquies—a being defining and redefining itself, learning how to know and endure itself, coming to understand the proper use of those solitudes within which we confront our own mortality.

Kirk's poems come to us embodied in a voice that is both

authoritative and authentic—there is in fact somebody at home in them, speaking. His poems sound like reports from what we understand as an actual world, and are thus mirrors in which we see ourselves actually reflected as we speak to ourselves.

Which does not mean that Kirk's work is attempting to sound especially "western" in some pseudo-archaic "cowboy" sense. It's just that it speaks in the common cadences of many lives in the West, reflecting on common anxieties and victories, sweetness and frailty, and the nine yards in between. Rather than being at all archaic, it's utterly contemporary. Life in downtown enclaves in Nevada, after all, can sometimes get a little more postmodern (self-reflexive and awash with disconnection and anomie) than anybody ever hoped—as in, for instance, *Leaving Las Vegas*.

As in, for instance, Kirk's poem called "The Misfits," in which we overhear Marilyn Monroe and Clark Gable talking over drinks in Reno while waiting to shoot the famous movie:

> *You know* she says *I walked out*
> *to the city limits once, it didn't*
> *look like much was out there*
>
> Clark kills his drink in one gulp
> motions to the bartender to bring
> them another round nods at her
> and says *Yeah, but it may be the*
> *only place there's anything left*

And then, essentially, like Kirk, they go to the desert to Fallon, leaving technicolor behind. As old friends of mine once said, "Walk away like a movie star." Which sounded great until it turned into a movie we lived out too often.

Locating made more sense than walking.

Increasingly, Kirk says, "the poems seem to be exploring the roles of place and perception in the formulation of notions of desire. What do we want? Why do we want it? What arouses our desire to stay 'here' rather 'there'?"

Kirk Robertson is a man whose work and way of speaking are centered in a particular kind of West, in the particularities of a certain place. He's securely located. But he's also seen some things, some disconnections. He brings us reports on the fracturing so many of us have suffered, and on the healing so many of us, all around, are beginning to think possible.

In Robertson's poems I hear the voice of a man who is speaking to himself as he goes on telling the story of who he is and who he loves, inventing and reinventing his way of connecting to the stranger inside, to the people he loves, and to the place where he feels at home.

Kirk Robertson's situation is our common situation; it is his courage and his willingness and ability to speak that are uncommon. His poems help us locate ourselves. That help is an invaluable gift.

WILLIAM KITTREDGE

Author's Note

Terry Allen once said, "Trying to talk about art is like trying to French kiss over the telephone." I feel pretty much the same about trying to talk about poetry. It's much better to read it. But, as this collection offers an overview of the past twenty-six years, I thought a few words regarding the structure and sequence of the collection might be appropriate.

This book represents a revision and expansion of a previously published, and now out-of-print selected poems, *Driving To Vegas* (1987). Two thematic, and more-or-less self-contained, sections in that book have been deleted and three new sections, poems written in 1987–95, have been added. With that exception this book represents an overview of my work between 1969 and 1995. Some of the earlier sections include poems that were not, for one reason or another, included in previously published books/chapbooks with the same title. These poems were written in the same place, around the same time as the others in those sections and seem to fit.

Although the poems, and the sections, are arranged in roughly chronological order, the organizing principle in grouping the poems is a kind of geography. Geography in the sense of landscape being both character and background, both external and internal, both *where* I was and how it felt to be there.

And, as someone has pointed out, the poet does not write the poem alone. Lingering below the surface you'll find art and artists, friends, women, the woman, and more than a little music—from Chopin to Cesaria Evora, Rimbaud to Leonard Cohen. The poems here also represent an attempt from the vantage point of late 1995 to indicate, as well as juxtapose, some ongoing concerns.

KIRK ROBERTSON
Fallon, Nevada
Winter 1995

Drinking

Beer

at

22

Below

Wheat Field with Crows, 1890

He played in the orchestra
first violin
second row

Never much considered
reincarnation before

Attending the Van Gogh
retrospective
at LACMA

The lines extended
around the block

And he felt
a certain ringing
in his ears

It was hot
102 and smoggy

When he saw a priest
walk down the street
disappear around
the turn of the century

Halloween

Eyes feel
like triangles
cut
with a kitchen knife
and removed
on a day
in October

It is difficult
to speak
of anything

Everything slopes
down
in every direction

Dancing
like a halloween
masque
of pregnant
pumpkins

That George C. Scott
would love
to devour
whole

Cracking the seeds
on his canines

Blues for a Brontosaurus

Muddy's blues on the radio
a wet emulsion
rain streaked windows
distant trees

Drinking wine
pushing smoke
zeroes out hoping
they add up
to something more

The only thing
that's closer
is tomorrow

It is skinnier
every day

Sail on my little honey bee
sail on

Just listen
to that harp

Humming along
like a drunken brontosaurus

I don't mind you sailin'
but puleeze
don't you sail so long

Small Ritual for Kerouac

Take two short dogs
of muscatel
down to the tracks
in the old
Westwood millyard

Stay
until the moon
comes up
over the ridge

Marvel at the clear
starlit night

Hear, coming out
Coyote howling
up at the end
of some lonesome
High Sierra road

The Clorox Kid

I scrubbed the floor
occasionally
I got called
on these jobs

Someone dying
got to be
too much of a mess
and the mess
must be disposed of

That's when
they called me

The angels of mercy
would rather not
soil those uniforms
and somebody
must clean up

I was resting up
for the nightly
nine o'clock
cardiac crapout
coupled with
overdoses
on this and that
when they wheeled
him in

He had drunk
Clorox
wishing
it was sweet
wine

Not just a sip
or two
but a whole
half-gallon

When I got there
to mop up
the entire ward
smelled
like Clorox

His liver was gone
the doctor too

Nothing to do
nothing
that could be
done

He sterilized
that room
simply
by dying in it

I punched out at eleven

In the morning
he was cut
into small squares
and they scoured
the walls
the sinks
the floors
with him

Punching in
the next day
even the time clock
exuded a soft Clorox hum
as I dipped my mop
in

And started scrubbing

Love Poems

Like the late worm
usually
miss the bird
entirely

Election Night

He comes in the door
fifth of Wild Turkey
ready to celebrate
even now two hours
before the polls
close talks about
the new job he'll
soon have depending
of course on the outcome
is particularly concerned
about how *I* voted says
I should support
and participate in
the greatest system
ever set up the one
Columbus brought over
Jefferson wrote down
and moved west to wipe
out the buffalo put him
in line for a thirty-nine
grand a year job
with the BIA it all
depends on Pennsylvania
he says then we'll know
but something about him
doesn't sit right growls
and snaps as Columbus
must have thankful for land
at last but knowing neither
where he's landed
nor where he's at

5:30 News

They ask the winos
if they're worried

"I think it's a woman
she dresses like a man"

"I don't sleep out no more
you betcha"

"You only gotta die once
God takes care of me"

They ask the police
if there are clues

The police are worried
they only know
it's a person
who carries a knife

They ask the winos
if they're worried
about the future

"What future?"

Seven dead
their throats slashed
in six weeks

The Slasher is loose
on the TV news

Arlee, Montana

Not much here
the two streets
squat like an X
in the wrong square
at the wrong time

Stepping out of the store
blood flooding the bed
of a pickup spilling
from the gutted eyes
of a five-point buck

Staring upward
into drifting snow
with no more answers
than I shudder
suddenly in the cold

The blood quickly
freezes
to ice
at twenty below

Owl

We get there first
let ourselves in
they come home later
ask if we saw Owl
on the roof—

*Last time we saw that
someone died maybe
you should stay over
another day*

We agree to stay
but they leave first
thing next morning
before the phone rings

A friend of theirs
a miscarriage she says
she wasn't pregnant

What can we do
I ask

Just tell them
she says

Hangs up

Maybe Owl was for her

Or maybe

Owl was for the miscarried one
the one who was not conceived
but who had something to say
and no way to do it

I think

Maybe that's what we stayed
an extra day to hear

Maybe that's why
they put canaries
in coal mines

The Mighty Hunter

Keeps at least one
loaded gun
in car shop
and house
just in case

Shoots at everything
that moves
and a lot
of what doesn't

Can hit two dimes
in the air
with a .22

Runs over
one afternoon
to ask
if anyone
wants a pet crow
he's just dropped
one somewhere out
in the road

Claims prowess
as a hunter
from his Indian
heritage

But something's
gone
his instincts
and those
of the animals
he claims
relation to
are crossed
like hairs
in the scope

They no longer
seem to understand
one another

He wonders where
all the jackrabbits
have gone why
when someone's dog
gets shot

They always think
he did it

A Discussion Concerning Lodging

He's the big Indian
trader an ex-smoker

You should have
seen it
he says

The car was bent
double

She had been cut
in half dead
instantly

The guy
with her
so drunk
he's sitting
on her
asking
for cigarettes

An old lady
walks in
with something
to sell

*I know
you're Indian*
she says
*you give me same
when I'm drunk
when I'm sober*

As she leaves
he looks back
at me
and my cigarette
and says

Your rent is due

Sunday Service at Short Bear's House

He was bundled up
sent off
to meet his father
the preacher
in the church
barely twenty yards
from the house

He wasn't missed
until his father
returned that evening
after services

They searched everywhere
all that day
into the next
found nothing
until

Goose Face
found him
four or five
miles northeast
of the church
frozen
dead
just a little
ways
from Short Bear's
house

I thought
I heard Coyote's crying
ten o'clock Sunday night
Short Bear said

A Letter to Boston

to bring in food, fresh meat
running blood down work
& laugh twisted faces
 —STUART Z. PERKOFF

You write of the Mandan
and the buffalo
both of which
are almost gone

I sit here
and try to write
between Indians
that come to the door
thinking I'm connected
with the trading post
to hock their radios
rifles and tape decks
numerous as the buffalo
were once fresh meat
for laugh twisted faces
almost as numerous
as Coyote's wine bottles
that fill the empty
lot in town with a glistening
green-white dance
shards
for some future
archaeological dig

Top Pieces for the Axis Nave

(a found poem)

Please untie
the wheels
of your car
and
respectively
put one top
piece
through
the middle
hole
of the rim

Then
mount
the wheels
again
tighten
as usually

Then
the top pieces
will be
fastened
unobjectionable

A Hole in One

On a tortuous switchback
outside Corpus Christi
tumbleweeds rambled up
and down the grade
passing cryptic greetings
almost inaudibly

As they rolled by
the local country club
the greens sang soprano

Notification of
surrounding communities
was slow in coming
horses rhinos tapirs
plugged the roads
in such numbers
that the concrete
finally gave out

Causing reputable
spokesmen
far and near
to pull their mustaches
into sand-cast yawns
over sixty fathoms deep
glistening with potassium

Gone in February

The dog's gone
run down by a chip truck

The wine's gone
bottle empty on its side

The smoke's gone
not even a butt

The lights have all gone
out in town

Even the water's going
out of the tub I filled
to drown the cold icy sleet

Outside the snow
inches down the Missions

Soon it will fill

Even this valley

Easter

It's spring
snow's melting
water running off
uncovers bodies
that have lain
for who knows
how long with
frozen hunks
of rainbow
in their hands

A schoolteacher
who didn't make it
to Sunday dinner
with her parents
is found
in her apartment
stripped
like a sun-bleached
skull the second
this week not much
for NY or LA
but unheard of
here in Missoula

Everything around us
seems to be ready
to surrender
to this notion
of death

Even the canceled
envelopes
of yesterday's mail
lie in the box
like spent white bodies
in a coffin waiting
to be opened

Everything that is
except a small patch
of grass in the alley
behind the post office
which so greenly explodes
and quietly rises
again

Snowing and in the Dark

It's dark
where I live
fully two months
into spring
and it's snowing

At the post office
there's a card
a bold red scrawl
that says
you're pissed off
about something

I try to read
through
your scrawl
try to see
what's going on

I imagine
dogs geese
teaspoons
perhaps snow
there too

But these images quickly fade
leaving just the anger
on the postcard

So
you're pissed off
there's nothing I can do
about that
or much of anything else
from here

I just wanted you
to know
how it feels
to stand in the reflectiveness

Of a snow covered parking lot
alone
with the bigness of the dark

And your card
the only one
in the box

A Quiet Man

He went out
hunting
while he was
gone
the soldiers
came
wiped out
his village
the old ones
the little ones
his mother

He returned
found
dead campfire
ashes
charred sticks
bits of skin
the bodies
of the slain
ashes and death
everywhere

He blackened
his face
with ashes
from a dead
campfire
sang
his song
of mourning
and set out

He searched
and searched
until he found
a trapper
he believed
was a member

of the tribe
that wiped out
his people

He wiped him
out

He was taken
by the soldiers
bound hand
and foot
he was *only*
an Indian
but the court
understood
his grief
so completely
that he was
only given
life
in prison

He believed
he was being
taken
to the home
of the white
tribe
to be wiped out
as they saw fit

He did not speak
he remained silent

He was insane
the government
believed
melancholia
so they
committed him

to the government
hospital

He waited
quietly
for his death

He did not
speak
for 32 years
he remained silent

Until some
of his tribe
visited
the hospital
and tried
to speak with him

He tried
to speak
but after
32 years
all he could say
was *ba-fo*

They spoke
to him again
this time
in the old
language
this time
he said

where is Three Bears?

The words
meant nothing
to him
but he knew
the wiped out
sign

and he understood
his visitors
when they
counted
26 snows

Fahrenheit 451 at 22 Below

It's cold outside
frozen stiff as I
watch a movie
about burning books

It's cold outside
on Highway 93
a cattle truck
roars by

It's cold outside
on TV the fire chief
says there's nothing
there—for peace
of mind
we burn it
the only way to be happy
is for everyone
to be made alike

It's cold outside
I could use some
of that heat she says
pointing at the TV screen
I'm going to bed

It's cold outside
on Highway 93
they have turned off
the EAT sign

It's cold outside
but on TV
Camus Dostoevski
the bedroom
even the fire chief
are going up in flames

It's cold outside
frozen stiff as I
look at the bookshelves

check the thermostat
and wonder if I am to die
in the snows of winter

Or if
as that old Japanese
soldier said
coming out of hiding
thirty years after
VJ Day

What difference does it make?

Shooting

at

Shadows,

Killing

Crows

Naming

HOW KILL TWO MOUNTED GOT HIS NAME

Surrounded
by the sound
of skulls cracking

He brought two Crows
down from the same horse

*   *   *

HOW MAN WHO SAW THE FIRST HORSE GOT HIS NAME

While crossing the river
he was the first
to see yellow
in the trees

*   *   *

HOW TRADER THAT BUILT A BAD HOUSE GOT HIS NAME

Staying behind
and using rotten wood

*   *   *

HOW LITTLE BEAVER GOT HIS NAME

Building a house
staying in it
most of the time

And being small

*   *   *

HOW FROZE ON THE PRAIRIE GOT HIS NAME

Looking for buffalo
being shot

And then freezing

*   *   *

HOW NOBODY CATCHES HIM GOT HIS NAME

Stabbing
his sister-in-law

*   *   *

HOW SHADOW GOT HIS NAME

From the shade
cast
by an umbrella

*   *   *

HOW BAD WITH WOMEN GOT HIS NAME

Building a house

Next to our
tipis

Sundance

Was held on Maggot Creek
where Appearing Wolf
killed seven
of Black Buffalo's
horses

And the whites called it
Sweetwater Creek

Captive

They took a white woman

They liked her
they would not give her up

They believed
she was good luck

Her waist was pinched
from wearing a corset

And they were impressed

Jealousy

Killing many of their own
horses

Just because they were
fatter

How the Treaty Was Signed

After giving us
a good time

And a keg of whiskey

What Caused Pimples on People's Heads

Hanging the two
who killed Spicer
when he wouldn't
sell them
whiskey

How the Missionaries Came

Traveling around the country

With a book

Measles

Camped on a bluff
with sore throats
faces broke out
with a bellyache

Eclipse

Turning black
dying
there

The sun

Winter

So cold
we got water
only
from beaver holes

So cold
that before they could
look in the tipis
for a place to stay
the crows fell
out of the sky

So cold
black bear
stayed with us
all winter
he was not
a friend

So cold
Buffalo Head
got dead

So cold
starving
around the kettle
eating each other

Found Frozen

Bent crazy
danced around
dragging
one foot
so that
like a wheel
his body turned
on the stump

Berdache

Hearing her husband
was killed
she hung herself

Swinging from a tree
the erection
of a man called Grass

Heyoka

Awaking with thunder
rolling in his head
every move he made
it got louder
and louder booming
off the inside
of his skull

He tried everything
it wouldn't stop
until
in his desperation
to get outside
he put his moccasins
on backwards
and suddenly

Silence

He found that
from then on
if he did everything
backwards
he never heard
that awful booming
in his head

But let him slip
just once
and there it was
crashing
in his ears

One day his
hunting party
was surprised
by the enemy
and outnumbered
six to one

He charged
into the enemy forever
silencing that awful
booming in his skull

Grief

Lone Horn after
accidentally
killing
his only son
mounted
his horse
vowed
to kill
the first
living thing
he met

His horse
came back
arrows
covered it
with blood

We followed
his tracks
back
found him
mangled
gored
by a buffalo bull

He had driven
his horse away
with arrows
killed the bull
with his knife

Death

HOW SAW THE BUFFALO WAS KILLED

By Crows
looking for buffalo

* * *

HOW SPREAD OUT WAS KILLED

Fingers
spread wide
on both hands
with an arrow

* * *

HOW SHOOTS RUNNING BEAR WAS KILLED

Stealing horses

Between the mouth of the Tongue
and the Powder

* * *

HOW LITTLE BEAR WAS KILLED

Coming to camp
under false pretenses
with a buffalo bone

* * *

HOW CAT OWNER WAS KILLED

Bleeding from nose
and mouth

By a spider web
thrown at him

* * *

HOW BROKEN LEG DIED

Finding whiskey
drinking it all
and puking

On his own stump

*   *   *

HOW HOLDING EAGLE DIED

Digging in a bank
for white clay

Which fell on him

*   *   *

HOW HAS THUNDER DIED

Living in a log house
without
sickness

*   *   *

HOW BIG LIPS DIED

Suddenly
in winter

*   *   *

HOW MONEY BOY DIED

With silver dollars
in his hair
dragged by horses
at the age of twelve

*   *   *

HOW HALF BEAR BODY DIED

Hanging

broken in two
just below the heart

*   *   *

HOW LITTLE GAY WAS KILLED

Measuring out
gunpowder
from the can

Smoking his pipe

*   *   *

HOW WORTH HAT DIED

In bed
burning gasoline
he thought was
kerosene

With two
other families

*   *   *

HOW JOE TOMAHAWK DIED

Leaning

His face over
a shotgun

*   *   *

HOW HAS A BOAT DIED

Resisting arrest

By the Indian police

*   *   *

HOW SILK'S WOMAN DIED

Shot in the head
accidentally

By Silk

Under

the

Weight

of the

Sky

Crossroads

One August afternoon
lost in Fallon, Nevada
at that point
when the sun
was still up
but the quality
of the light on the hills
suddenly changed
and it seemed
somewhat cooler

He realized
that he could never
forget all that needed
to be forgotten that
he was left
with only a few things
trips and places
that mattered

That he named them
like streets
to convince himself
not so much
that he knew
where he was going
but that at least
he knew where he was

He'd been in the middle
of a warm period
but the next ice age
was already 2,000 years
overdue even the armadillos
were moving south
from Nebraska to Mexico
the land was getting
colder and colder
temperatures marched

farther south every year
soon even here the roads
would be covered with ice
until late in the afternoon

5:22 A.M.

At this degree of light
I can just barely see

Get up and piss

Light a cigarette
look out the window

Listen to the wind
rattle the trailer

Light another

Sit next to a humming
electric heater
wait for the light
to disclose the chaos

Unlike out there
where it's all
covered smoothly
in white blankets
without warmth

Dead Dog

It was a bitch
putting her down
ground frozen
hard full of rocks

Two weeks later
Christmas
he got *Call of the Wild*
aftershave in a bottle
shaped like a dog

Thank you he said
thinking about
how many times
he said that

How many times

he was given
what he didn't
really want

How many times
he said thank you
for it

Titanic

They've been there
over two hours
these young kids
hitchhiking
guy in gray
with frizzy hair
redhead in black t-shirt

They get no rides
only a drunken Indian
slows down the sun
pushes things above
ninety in the shade
with not a cloud
to offer any

They sit on their packs
she takes out a flute
plays *Nearer My God to Thee*
and I think
now, that's style
but when he takes
out a harp
does a few Bob Dylan riffs
I'm not so sure

Apparently she's not either
she's packed up and is
walking across the street
to Burgertown like a rat
leaving a sinking ship

Thanx for the Drinks Ladies

We picked them up
hitchhiking
outside San Berdoo
they were going to Vegas
and so were we

We drove on out
into the desert
getting up to speed
popping beers

Jim was spinnin' out
get-rich-quick schemes
to the skinny one

We descended
into the lights
tried to find
a friend
a dealer
but he'd punched
out his pit boss
been fired

If you take us
to Caesars
we can get
some money
the pudgy one said

We sat at the bar
watched
this guy peel
off several hundred
and give it
to them

We followed them out
at a discrete distance
having been warned
not to look like
we're with them

I know this motel
let's go there
the rooms are cheaper
the pudgy one said
back in the truck

They paid for the room
and went up
Jim went to the liquor store
came back with a fifth of JD

They were getting ready
long tight black dresses
cleavage big hair
tons of makeup
when we came in

Jeezus thanx for the drinks
the skinny one said

I sat on the bed
watching the skinny one
pull on her stockings
listening to Jim
and the pudgy one
making plans

Now we'll go out
and turn a couple
tricks she said

Then we can go
out to this cabin
on the lake
and relax

They called a cab
swished out the door
with lipsticked goodbyes
and see-you-laters

We finished the fifth

Jim rifled the purse
they'd left behind
took out enough
to cover the whiskey

And a tube of lipstick
Thanx For The Drinks Ladies
the mirror said
as we closed the door
the sun was coming up

Birthday

It's been hot

But then it's mostly
always hot
in Nevada
in the summer

The days are removed
one at a time

I sit very still
in front of the cooler
drink beer

I've just convinced myself
that it's not that bad
that it *could* be worse
when she shows up
and begins
to tell me
her version
of the news

It's time to go
I tell her
drive to town
drop her off
at a small cabin
the screen torn
where her air
conditioner hangs

I drive
past polar bears
caged in glass
kangaroo rats
run headlong
under the wheels

I get back
remove my boots
one at a time
look at the holes
in my socks
in the first day
of my 29th year

It's Like Putting on Your Hat
While Reaching Out for Your Ears

Some make it by teaching college
by embracing some theory of cosmic unity
some make it with dope
or booze or both
some make it with Christ
some make it by making it with everybody
by making babies
by throwing pots
or the *I Ching*
some make it without meat
eggs milk or other dairy products
some make it by throwing up
by sailing a ship of flowers through Suez
some make it by slashing Rembrandts
some make it by running
some by standing still
some make it by hiding
some make it by opening a beer
next to an open window
in a freeway motel
some make it quietly
alone and unnoticed
some make it

And some don't

The View

They tell you
it's something
you'll enjoy
promise you
a night of laughs
tomorrow

But the way
things look
out your window
off your
porch
it's not
at all surprising

That people
jump
or put it
to the wall
with one
final blast
of laughter

Larry Moon

I was smart they said
so they put me up
a couple of grades
which got me out
of grammar school early
it was just too rough
too many of the wrong
kind my mother said
the local junior high
wasn't for me
so she sent me off
every day
in a big yellow bus
full of gray uniforms
on their way to
Hawthorne Christian School

Where I met Larry Moon
held back a couple of grades
and tough real tough
he'd been kicked out
of the same junior high
that was too tough for me
while lighting a cigarette
one day after school
he let the match go out
I called him a motherfucker
he split my lip
and cocked to fire again
screaming *what's it mean*
what's it mean
as I stood there
speechless bleeding
scared shitless
I was smart they said
but I didn't know
I just didn't know

A Stitch in Time

Riding around Provo
on a bicycle this car
suddenly alongside
high school jocks
yelling running
him off the road

The chain slips
the sprocket catches
his foot neatly spearing
flesh from bone blood
oozing out and over

They drive off
laughing

He manages
to get the chain
back on manages
to ride leaving
a trail behind him
like Hansel and Gretel
to a friend's house
where with the help
of some methiolate
and a little whiskey
he begins
to stitch things up

Omen

It's so hot even
the rattlesnakes
are moving
across the agency
toward the river

It's been over
a hundred for
over a week

Guests and chaos

Not exactly
The Day of the Locust
but there are two strange
Cricket lighters
on my table

She says my hands
are like branding irons

Do you believe that
I ask her

I believe that
I might walk out
and something could
happen to me, yes
she says

A Reply

She says she keeps on
writing
because I haven't
told her not to

I've spoken to the rain
and it didn't do any good

She writes that she's going
to school studying a lot
seeing psychics
seeking help with things
putting the past
into the present

She says if she knew
then what she knows
now she'd really like
to know what I think
of it all

Sometimes I think
all people can do
doesn't make any difference
it all comes
from inside *here*
is the center
like the hubcap
on a wheel
that the sun's rays
shine from
when not obscured
by clouds
or spattered with mud

So, look,
I can't see anything
I have nothing to say
or write

So don't

Last Dance

I don't know why
there has been who

In the end
I'm always alone
in the dark
with just the music

Dancing like a fool
who believed
in something
he can no longer
follow

Olympics

We're all skiers
on a downhill run
rushing madly
past the ones
who've fallen
the course
getting faster
harder to hold
hoping we don't
catch an edge
hoping we get
down
the right words
before
the finish

Ketchup in Ketchum

Gene asked me
to lay a flower
on his grave
which isn't much
a rectangle of concrete
the name a couple dates

A black bird
in a nearby tree
yelling and diving
at my head
everytime I tried
to get close enough
to lay the weeds
I'd gathered
on the tombstone

I finally managed
to get the blossoms
down
and left

Driving north out of town
I hit a dog ran right
under the wheels
nothing I could do
but hunt around
until I found
his people
deliver him
still alive
at least

Then stop
by the Salmon River
wipe the dried blood
from the car seat
looking kinda' like

spilt ketchup
dried on the drainboard
or on last week's dishes
still waiting there
to be washed clean
and laid in the cupboard

Lovelock to Twin Falls

All along even here
in some of the most
barren places
imaginable
you see them
these abandoned
shacks
rock tin and weathered wood
where someone thought
things would work out
and they tried
failed
and moved on

Twin Falls to St. Ignatius

The last big push have
to be back at work day
after tomorrow all night
radio station drifting
in and out some rain
over Lost Trail
the lights of Missoula

Postcard to My Unborn Son

I just thought
since you're all curled up
inside there
I'd tell you about it
how it was
when your mother and I
came together

In a moon of cherries
Squirrel ran up a tree
Wind blew but stopped
when the pipe was lit
and the breath trapped
in small buckskin pouches

I was told *you will
have a tough life*
all you can do
is go through it

And that's how small things
survive like grass
pushing up through
cracks in the asphalt

Finish High School

Nine A.M. and I
have to be there
at work I
go to pick up
the parts

There's two
old black guys
60 or so
putting molding
on the door

One holds
the molding
the other drives
the nail

The first one
misses
to the outside
they trade
the other
misses
to the inside

Fuck it says the first

I dunno says the second

They light cigarettes
I light a cigarette
it says FINISH HIGH SCHOOL
on the matchbook

The older
of the black guys
puffs and puffs
steps back and says
this is the way
to do it and

pulling a nail
from his pocket
splits the molding
in half

The other guy says
pulling another nail
from his pocket
fuck it and
secures the other half

As I finish my coffee
the first the older
black guy
comes over and says

Some days they work
Some they don't

Moldings
or frames
of reference
I'm not sure

But I suppose
he knew both
equally well

Gladioli

I

I've seen red
ones yellow ones
and white ones
possibly pink but
I'm not sure

II

They always seem to be
present at weddings
and funerals

III

They masquerade
as pumpkins and gourds
on Halloween

IV

They turn into
unmatched socks
when left behind
in laundromat dryers

V

Van Gogh found them
difficult
to work with
turned to sunflowers
as models

VI

They are tall
or at least seem
to be pulled
up quite high
on thick green ropes

VII

When I was a kid
the thought that
these giants
lingered
in my grandmother's
backyard
terrified me

VIII

There are at least
35 of them
outside this window
right now
growing closer
all the time

IX

They grow from bulbs
and come back
in the spring
like snakes
uncoiling

X

Their name means
small sword

XI

Rimbaud went to Abyssinia
and smuggled them

October and Not Much Relief in Sight

The country's almost
two hundred and rusting
I'm almost thirty
as women in housedresses
across the country
worry about their fat
their husbands
and lovers
linger over
pool tables
in corner bars
moths walk the ceiling
of this room
and outside
someone slides
under
the wheels
of a log truck
in the rain
that has almost
filled
that empty
Folger's can
out there
in the weeds

Incompetent Psychedelic Rotogravure

The national spelling bee
is on TV
I watch them
go through the words
cucaracha
brilliantine
and the winner's word
incisor

Once I went through
Fallon
stopped to see
her dying
grandmother
she was thin
old dying not
really there
but we talked
for a while
then I left
it was time
for her
lunch

Once in sixth grade
I won
a spelling bee
the word was the one
with a rat
in the middle
separate

And that's how
she died
six months later
alone
I imagine her teeth
like a rat's were
yellow

Petroglyphs

Small tracks in the rock
niches and backbones
of snakes

Pieces chipped and taken
beer cans soda cans styrofoam

The sun sets
over rocks too hard
to incise

The mosquitos come
suddenly over the rock
that says
NO DEAD ANIMAL DUMPING

The tracks in the rock
flicker and recede
into the car away
from the mosquitos

All I can see
out the windshield
is a solitary bat
flying over out
there into the dying
light spots
afterimages
mark his path
small tracks
across the sky

The smog has reached
even here

Montauk Cafe

It's a small cafe
the only one
on the reservation
open this time of day

I order coffee
the Indian cop
eats breakfast
the White cop
comes in
orders coffee

Wish us White folks
could eat like that

Yeah

We can't get any
commodities
but you damn Injuns can

Yeah
and he adds
under his breath
you bastard

I stay a half-hour
until the record
starts to play over

Wish us White folks . . .

But they have agreed

That Nixon is useless
as tits on a mule

That they haven't
seen Bob drunk
in quite a while

That there's nothing
to do

And plenty of time
to do it in

My Father

I didn't know him
very well he and
my mother split up
and I only saw him
when he came to town
once a year at
the Capri Motel
next to LAX

Then I moved out
and even that stopped

I was 22 or 23
when I next heard
from him

A hastily written
note on a half-sheet
of yellow paper

Dear Kirk it said
I guess I haven't been
much of a father
and perhaps
I've developed
a jaundiced attitude
toward things
but I've tried to do
what I thought
I had to

I mentioned the letter
to my mother
he's just *got* jaundice
she said from all
his drinking

I meant to go see him
or at least write
but the draft board
was on my ass
and I never did

About four years
after that letter
they found him
in his old clunker
in Santa Ana
as dead as the battery

Ice Lines

In this dream
the other night
her fingernails
grew and grew
just kept
growing
and I saw
death streak
the sky

But I awoke
in the morning
to her fingernails
the same except
her hair was red
outside the brown
hills were white now
the air cracked
like an ice cube
in warm bourbon

The news is slow
to reach me
in Montana
in winter
but there is something
here and perhaps
there too

That I hope
I have not destroyed
that I hope
is still here

Alive

Making Reservations

Some are there
because they're wild

Some are there
because they're
very destructive

And some are there
because they
had no room

Green concrete blocks
chain-linked cells
with numbers

The floor smelling
and slippery
their eyes sad
and questioning
not really understanding
wild or destructive
the inability
to get along
or our staring eyes
just the lack of room
and the scent of death
three days away

Most are there
because they were simply
no longer wanted

I've seen the same eyes
in bus stations
and corner bars

0 and 2

Baseball Paul
walks up and down
the streets of Arcata
the main ones
there are only two
up one
back down the other
all day long
every day
walking
and talking
baseball cap
pulled low
over ragged
flannel
and tennis shoes
pounding his mitt
asking as you pass
wanna play some ball
wanna play some ball
pulling the cap lower
hiding those eyes
that have seen
too may curves
taken too many strikes

The Letter

She gets a letter
from an old friend

He's in a bad way

She reads the letter
and then
I read the letter

What do you think
she asks

I say
what I think

She thinks like the moon
rising she can light
his darkness

I say
you could phone him

But she's reading
Dear Abby
looking for advice
I suppose

So I look out the window
at the sun that sets
earlier every day soon
it will snow here
bright white like the moon
a false reflected light
only one side with warmth

Vietnam

I was close
to three who went
two came back

One sits in a ten-by-ten shack
watching a leased color TV
twelve or fourteen hours a day

He's three months behind
on the rent
but up on the TV payments

He comes home
on his lunch hour
to watch a quick half-hour
shoot some darts
at the John Wayne army
recruiting posters
that hang on the wall

You don't expect it
he asks
to make any sense
do you

The other talks about it
constantly
can't seem to talk
about anything else

How's it goin'
I ask

OK he says
but this one time
in country
we captured some VC
and they took this one
I think he was a captain
in the NVA up

in a helicopter
a thousand feet or so
and kicked him out

Have you ever seen
a watermelon
hit the ground
he asks
just splatters everywhere

It seems to have done
something
to all of us
but I notice it
most in those
who've been there
and come back
alive
but not quite right

An insanity we share
along with the weight of the sky

Origins,

Initiations

Birth

Perhaps

Raven formed the world

Filled it
with animals
birds
fish
everything

Got it
ready
for people

Then fucked a stone
and an elderberry bush
at the same time

A great deal
depended
on who
gave birth
first

If Stone
people would
have scales
all over
and would not die

If Bush
people would
have only
finger and toe
nails
and would
sooner or later
die

Bush
gave birth
first
to people
with nails
sorrow sickness
and death

Stone
saw bush
deliver
and stopped
bearing

Thus ending the matter

Fire

Lizard sunning on a rock
was first to see it
falling from the sky

Coyote identified it
as an ash

Hummingbird found
the direction
in which to go

Coyote stole it
with a wig
of milkweed string

Coyote passed it
to Jackrabbit

Jackrabbit burned
his tail black
carrying it

Rat heard him
squealing
and took it
put it
in a pile of brush
which he threw
everywhere

The brush
now has
Fire

You let it out
with a drill

Salt

Used to be far away
from everyone

He was a man
back then
traveling around
the country

People never
used him

He was ugly
all over

They didn't like
that

He'd come into
a camp
and say *hey*
let me
put my hand in there
it'll taste so good

But people took
one look
and always said
I don't think so

They were going
to eat it
and he was
just flat out
too ugly

Or *no*
your hand is much
too dirty

Finally though
he found some

who were willing
to let him
put his hand
in their food

And he did so

And they tasted it
and it was good

So good that
from then on
Salt stayed
right there

Where he may
be found

Even today

Snakes

Some believe snakes
were once
like everyone else
with bodies
with arms and legs
but then

They decided
to live
in the caves
of the world
below this one
and changed
their shape
to do so

Losing
their arms
and legs
gave them power
over death
they were not
afraid
to die
in winter

They came back
in the spring
like other
seeds
bulbs
roots

Marriage

While still in the world
somewhere below
this one
two couples married

And rubbed the skin
from their bodies

Rolled it
into a ball
and placed it
on the ground

Then they sat
around it
and sang
shaking rattles
until

A youth appeared

Dancing

Assholes

While traveling
around
Dog
came upon
the people
who had no
assholes

He wondered
how they could
ease themselves
after eating

They ate only
steam inhaled
from the cooking food

They cooked men

Dog
getting hungry
killed one
of their horses
a mountain goat
and ate it

Then he went out
and took a shit

One of the people
saw him
thought
it was great

So before long
each and every
one of them
wanted an asshole

They called Dog
over and carefully

examined his ass

They said
they were going
to make themselves
holes
too

And they punctured
this one
with a knife

He died

Dog ran off

Having no desire
to stay

With these people

Babble

He got tired of everyone
saying he was good
for nothing
so one day
he changed
into Eagle
went and lived
on a high steep
mountain

He came down
every day
but only to kill
people

Something
had to be done

So Little Man
decided he
would kill him
and he went up

Eagle was away
only his wife
was home

You must hide she said
it is time for Eagle to come

Quickly Little Man
changed into a fly
and hid
under a pile
of dead bodies

Soon Eagle came
with more
dead bodies
he ate
then lay down
to sleep

Little Man
came out
cut off
Eagle's head

He poured
warm water
over the bodies
and they came
back to life

But some of them
had been there
too long
they had turned
white

And when Little Man
tried to speak
with them
they spoke

A different
language

Wind

Some say Wind
That Was
gave them life

The Wind That
Is Now
coming out
of our mouths
gives us
life

When it
ceases
to blow
we die

We see
in the skin
at our fingertips
a trail

Wind That Was
blew
at our ancestors'
creation

Others say
Wind
is the sound
of many legs
coming
over the mountain

Scratch Shot

Wolf and Coyote had been uptown
drinking most of the day
ever since they found
that fifth of Canadian Club
at the dump

Now they were trying
to shoot a game
of eight ball
but mostly just
arguing

Wolf said
  people die twice
  they must die twice

Coyote said
  that's not right
  that's bullshit
  I don't want people
  to die twice
  once is enough

Then dropped the eight ball
in the side pocket

Wolf went home
and bewitched Coyote's boy

And Coyote said
  Wolf
  when will my boy
  get up to die again
  you said people
  should die twice

Wolf Said
  oh but don't you
  remember when
  you said that
  they should die
  only once

How to Join the Little Fire Fraternity

Plunge your arm
up to the elbow
in hot coals
light corn husks
eat them

Be able to see
into your body
let Cougar
Bear Badger or Wolf
live there

Be torn
limb from limb
your arms and legs
thrown into the fire

Rise in one piece
in perfect condition

Take the hearts
from butterflies
dragonflies
mix them
with roots
and blossoms
drink the sun
then

Sit around and bullshit

How to Join the Ant Fraternity

Go over
the southern road
to Red Ant's hills

Step firmly
on a deserted hill
extend your right
foot
over the hill

Stand on your toes
stoop over
the hill
and pray

Use a broom
to sweep away
from the sick
naked body
showers
of pebbles
shot into it
by ants
who've been
brought
to the surface
angered

At being stepped
and pissed on

How to Join the Rattlesnake Fraternity

Accidentally

Step
on a bowl of medicine

Break it
spilling
the medicine

Turn over
a carving
of Rattlesnake
into
the medicine

Bathe it

How to Join the Spiral Shell Fraternity

Sprinkle piss
on a heated stone
crush medicine over it

Don't fail
to undo
the knots
by rolling it
in your hands
until it drops
in four pieces
at your feet

Stay in your house
four weeks
before wearing
the mask
or it will stick
to your skin
break it
drive you crazy
you'll die
in four days

Have your nose
pierced
an eagle plume
inserted
while blood
is lapped
from the wound
by your brothers

Don't fuck
for a year afterwards

Then capture Wood Rat
roast him eat him
so that your blood
might be pure

When you start

How to Join the Eagle Down Fraternity

Paint your feet and legs
to the knees
and your hands and arms
to the elbows
white

Don't eat
animal food
or grease

Cure the sick
by dancing

How to Join the Fraternity That Does Not Fast from Animal Food

Never
eat Jackrabbit
instead
be able
to hold

A hot coal

In your mouth

How to Join the Hunters' Fraternity

Play with live coals
rub them
on your body

Kill your prey
by smothering it

Then wash its blood
from your hands
over the fire

With water
from your mouth

How to Join the Cactus Fraternity

Kill an enemy
but don't
take the scalp

Be cured
of a wound
arrow bullet
or dog bite

Be struck
by flying cactus
at an outdoor
ceremony

Don't fuck
for five days
after joining

Or cactus needles
will fill
your flesh

How to Join the Galaxy Fraternity

Have medicine so strong
that if taken alone
your intestines will burn

Be able to eat shit
drink piss

Decorate yourself
with mud
from the spring

Travel with laughter

Eat the most
bits of old blankets
splinters of wood

Bite the heads
from living mice
chew them tear dogs
limb from limb
fight over the liver

Eat the intestines

How to Join the Sword Swallowers Fraternity

Don't eat sweets
beans squash
peaches or coffee
only game

Don't fuck
for four days

Be able to freeze
the corn
if you dance
in summer

Be able to swallow
a sword
from middle fingertip
to elbow
in length
while dancing

Then drink whiskey
and watch

For the morning star

How to Join the Struck by Lightning Fraternity

Survive

Reasons

and

Methods

Smoke

Raising my pipe
a bubbling spring
comes
from hard ground

The flame
goes up
to my body

I rise from
the flowing
spring and walk
around the sky

It's easy

Come on

Go with me

Almost Like a Breeze

Sometimes
late at night
after the moon
has finally gone
and it is quiet

You can hear it

The sound of laughter
and talking

Coming from way off
over there
bouncing
almost like a breeze
across the desert floor

The sound of Coyote
and that darn fool
Rabbit

Probably drinking again

Doing pretty much
the same things
we do

Only better

The Bone Game

Everybody got together
for the celebration

Rabbit and Wolf
suggested the bone game

And they sat down

Wolf held the bone
sang

> *very very soon*
> *your intestines*
> *will be hanging out*

> *and I'll go*
> *right between your ears*

But Rabbit won anyway

So Rabbit took the bone
sang

> *I see*
> *I see a hole in the wall*

> *that's where I'll go*
> *if I'm attacked*

Then Deer sang
saw herself floating
downstream
past a log jam

But the game went on

Proverb

Going to get them
would be like
buying a salmon's asshole

Charm

Take a spider web
spun over the mouth
of a hole in the ground

Remove it carefully

Leaving in trade
cotton red rock pollen
deer or rabbit meat

Take the web
place it in the house
in some place
where
she'll be sure
to touch it

Then go home

And sing
butterfly songs
as long as you
can

Advice

Even a toothless deer
can do something so

You're not the only one
with a mind

To think so
would be taking
the corner of a house
for the door

And you don't want to die
with all your teeth
still in your head

Do you?

Hunt

A low tree is fired
near the base
with a torch

Rabbit sticks
are passed
through the flames

The rabbits are killed
left to be
picked up
by young girls
who run
get them
and return
to the circle

The first rabbit killed
has its nose cut
is handed
to someone
who just might carry
her heart in her rattle

And she rubs
the bleeding nose
down along the inside
of her thighs

Relations

My year-and-half-old son informs me
that the birds sing like Indians
do around a drum

Cultural Anthropology

I'm sitting
in the sun
reading
feeling pretty good
spring and all
when they
run up

Four or five
years old
one Indian
one White

Whatcha doin'
they ask

Readin'

Whereya from
they ask

Here
where you from

From Medford
Oregon
the White one
says

From my momma
the Indian one
says

Wohaws

Are what they demanded
as payment
for crossing their land

Soon the Whitemen
the cattlemen
began to reckon
the cost of a trip west
in Wohaws

The first ones
they saw
were teams of oxen
pulling
the Whiteman's wagons

And they listened
to what
they were called

Over and over again

Whoa!
Haw!

Teddy Blue Abbot's Recipe

Take one barrel
of Missouri River water
and two gallons of alcohol

Add two ounces of strychnine
to make them crazy
two bars of tobacco
to make them sick
because they wouldn't
figger it was good
unless it did
and five bars of soap
to give it a bead

Then add a half-pound
of red pepper

Put in some sagebrush
boil until it's brown

Strain this into a barrel

You've got
your basic Indian whiskey

Saturday Night, St. Ignatius, Montana

Their relations circled buffalo
circled Custer into oblivion

But here on the reservation
in their Mustangs and Pintos
all they circle is Burgertown

The bumper stickers read
THE LITTLE BIGHORN, CUSTER BLEW IT
CUSTER WORE ARROW SHIRTS
and the buffalo
are all down the road

In the National Bison Range

What She Did with the Silverware
Given to Her by a U.S. Congressman
Desiring to Civilize & Christianize Them

Gave the knives
to anyone
who wanted
to make carvings

Used the large
silver spoons
for popcorn water

Gave the forks
to children
as playthings

And returned

To using her fingers

Why There Is No Longer a Perpetual Fire
Kept in the Kiva
Of Any Pueblo

They've found the way
to the woods

Clear of enemies

And matches

Of Course There Are Many Different Versions of This Story, But . . .

You know I can get
into my car and drive
across my reservation
in about fifteen minutes
the Paiute said

Well if I get
into my car the first thing
in the morning and drive
all day that night
I'll be at the end
of my reservation
the Navajo said

Yeah the Paiute replied
I had a car like that
once

Desire

Yellow Pine's brother Bull Pine
had this hankering after
Post Oak's sister Black Oak

He wanted her
in the worst way

And soon

He was even ready
to marry her

Her father Water Oak
said *Sure, sure, go ahead*
if you want to

But her mother Brush Oak
wouldn't hear of it
kept shaking back and forth
saying *no, no, no*

They had just come together
all in the same place
to talk it over
when Coyote

Drunk again
and burning rotten logs

Let Fire get away
from him

Powers

Spirits
the sun
moon and stars
the Katsina
rainmakers
the cardinal
points

Breath
clouds
airplanes

Anything
we don't
know

Yet

Mole and the Sky

Mole's ashamed to come out
in the daytime for anyone to
see his huge hands

You see once
the sky fell and he held it
with his hands turned bottom up
under the weight of the sky

So now he hardly comes out
at all preferring instead
the dark tunnel of his own vision
scooped out with those huge hands

And if he does

It's only at night when he cannot
see it all happening again cannot
feel the pressure of those billowing
white clouds on his hands

False Spring

I'm afraid only
of the wind
when the trees sing
sitting alone
and owls

But I still
go around
pitying myself

My eyes searching
for signs of summer
in mid-March

Spell

—*for Valerie*

We have come together
somewhere out in the desert
miles from the reasons and methods
by which we measure such things

You are Deer and I
am probably Wolf
but I am not sure

But I do know
that I will take your body
eat it swallow you
your spit still fresh

I will wrap your heart
in the web
of an almost black spider
coming and going
never feeling any loneliness

And all of this will be done
secretly at night
while you are sleeping

You will never know

I will rub *my* spit
just below the curve
of your breasts and
that should do it

But even if it doesn't
there are other ways

Now

That we've come together

I-80

Headed

West

Powwow

Six A.M.
Fourth of July
Indians follow
the sound of the drum
the gardener next door
follows the sound
of his lawnmower
back and forth
these sounds beat
finally cutting
the threads
of what it is
I've been up
all night trying
to piece together
it was the loudest
thunder we've ever
heard the Rainbow
People tell me on
the way back from
their gathering
of the Blackfeet's
medicine that drove
them out tipis almost
lifted off the ground
into a sky that minutes
before had been limp
as a flag on a hundred
and three degree day
in a car outside
Browning Montana
eleven Indians
went off the road
coming back
from a powwow
eight were killed

the doctor tells me
that nothing starts
till ten here
on the reservation

Running Low

Realizing that I have lived
in at least fifteen different
places in three states over
the past eight years
not counting the innumerable
trips to here and there
and now feeling tired
running low but still
not feeling like I'm
in the right place
the chosen one and once
again feeling like moving on
I remember Kerouac heading
west on a train with everyone
out there reading *On the Road*
wondering just how and why
and where he'd missed the exit
not knowing how far it was
to the next one not knowing
why there never seemed to be
a place with enough space
to stop for a while
the shoulder of the road
barely wide enough
to pull over
for a piss stop

Movin' On

I've known dreamers
I've known fools sometimes
hard to tell
between the two

I've seen them come
on the scene burning
seen them go
various ways
some glamorous
some not so

All with their own
degrees of pain

Some were shot down
by bullets
by their faith
in the revolution
in their friends
in any number of things
that at one point
or another
ceased to work

They turn to Christ
they turn to a job for security
they turn to needles
they turn to ecologically
feasible alternatives
they seem to turn away
from a certain kind
of life

They turn into something
I can't understand
something that no longer writes
I mean even letters

All these so-called
old friends from school

Turn into something
I no longer bother
trying to call
when I get to town

Morningland

Haven't seen her in years
but ran into her somewhere
south of LA she owns
a health food store
member of a religious
commune something like that
has friends with names
like Karass and Dharma
who all wear airbrushed
t-shirts and order margaritas
without tequila when we go
out for dinner
at the Mexican place

Note to a Painter

I found it interesting
that you labeled my comments
pointless that same word
echoed here in this early
coffee morning book review

Perhaps you are stuck

I am not

Even though I too
have often found
most things
pointless dull
the knife never sharp
enough to pierce the skin

But there have been times
when the cut was so quick
so deep that a bold crimson
swatch splashed across
the page and the taste
was oh so incredibly sweet

But they were hard to see
you had to move quickly
to catch them had to listen
even when you knew
there was no point
in filling in the canvas

Which is what I suppose
John Thomas was getting at
when he pointed out
that the difference
between painters and poets
is that the latter
do not have to
keep their hands still

Nevada

The Milky Way
probably sits
out there
like a dotted
line stripe
down a skunk's
back or on
a paved road

The stars bob
like canoes
going over the falls
swept along
by the current
too late to stop
only the moon

Comes up
like a grapefruit
yellow yard light
in the Nevada desert

Coyote nuzzles the buck
hanging in the tree
and runs off
when I open the door

To look for stars

Pecan Pies

It must have been at least
twenty-five years ago
in a small town in Texas

He used to sneak into
this old man's backyard
fill paper bags
with pecans he
being the youngest
slower than the rest
was always the one
that got caught
had to stand there
while the old fool
dumped his nuts
on the ground
stomped them

Now all these years later
on a shelf in Safeway
in a small Nevada town
there it is
seems like the first
pecan pie he's seen
since then

Even though it's too much
he buys it takes it home
cuts a slice and finds only
a few pecans scattered
here and there on the top

Other than pecan pies and himself
which both seem a little less
the years have changed nothing really

Out the window the same cold wind
whips up memories like dust devils
then blows on over a barren landscape
leaving nothing where once it seemed
there had been something

Goin' to the Post Office with My Son

We do it six times a week
he really likes it yells
flag flag flag
when we get there
runs right on in

While I open the box
dig it out
he climbs the stairs
to those rarely visited
second-floor offices

He sits at the top
waits for me to ascend
and open the day's catch

There's lots of books
and mags in there
there are two checks
totaling $4.80
there is one acceptance
four rejection
slips in there

While I read through them
he says *hi* to everyone
underneath passing by
then we come down
hand in hand
headed home
for the Sunday layover

Visitor

His knock rattles the door
so I get up and let him in

Listening to him
is like getting stoned
with a bunch of old friends
you haven't seen
in a long time

You can hear the energy
the sound of lightning
somewhere in the air
a bright flash
for a moment or two
but nothing really there
through all that
distance

Spiral

Watching Dick Clark
count toward the new year
Times Square at 20 below
the baby falls
into the crowd
everybody cheering
yelling

Here it's the sound
of firecrackers
one or two quick
rifle shots
a little early
according to
Dick's countdown
and it's all over

I switch off the TV
crawl under the covers
the yard light outside
coming through the blinds
the sound of a sonic boom
cracking the black Nevada
night like a nutshell
spiraling away from me
faster and faster
like a dimly remembered event
from my childhood some toy
broken so many years ago

Dry Spell

The worst drought
in these here parts
old timers say
in eighty-five years

And then

Yesterday

More rain
than we've had
all year

Everything's flooded
buckets
under holes
in the roof

Outside
the truck's
stuck in wet sand

Like the words
in my head

Spinning

Going nowhere

A Dark Night

I don't know why
cigarette smoke finds the eye
why I seem to know no more
than the owl about how
or why the stars sit
above me why I sing
like birds only at
sunrise or sunset
the points of change
of contact between
the light and the dark
seem to be the ones
with the most interest
the ones to be looked at
understood that certain
things can never be
understood why we take
the chance is simply
beyond my grasp
twinkling overhead
holding out
a false promise

Monday Night, Lovelock

Realize it's hard
to move on
in the desert
but certain shortages
force you to try

Understand
that things
like drowning
in the desert
will sometimes happen

Drive around
looking at the junk
people let pile up
around their houses
as if somehow
the sheer accumulation
of broken senseless
sun-bleached things
will fill the spaces
in their lives
like the moon
does the night

Wait till
it comes up
listen to Coyote
ask that cool yellow disc
for *relief* for *release*

Go back
to the motel
switch on the cooler
swat a few mosquitos
swirl the ice
in your glass
settle down
and watch
the Giants and Cubs
slug it out

Without Apparent Cause

All of a sudden things
fall apart without apparent
or other cause slip
from your grasp your palms
not even wet as if you'd
never really held anything
at all

Things spiral away
from your control
are sucked back
before you know it
you are two years old
trying to hold on
to a piece of bread
while surrounded
by four barking dogs

Not knowing that you hold
the why and the wherefore
right in your own hand

For a little while
at least

Drumstick for Cody

I found a stick
that would do

It was a little longer
than necessary
but you will grow

Scrounged up
an old towel
cut it
in three-inch strips

Covered them
with white buckskin
stitched that down
with waxed thread
splitting the excess
for fringe

Cut more fringe
for the handle
adding some brass tacks
and two wing feathers
from a magpie
Uncle Adze shot

And it was done

I hope it
gives you songs
that glide
like a hawk
out the kitchen window
all those clouds
and sky behind them

Badlands

It's the way
things have
of going nowhere
running dry
hovering
like a fly
with no place to land
finding not what
allured you
in that first pass
only what threatens
to remain without relief
a rattlesnake coiled
under a rock
hungry and alone
miles from water
the insensate blue
of the sky beats down
buzzards circle
the sun dry bed
of a river too
long forgotten
these are indeed
badlands
a flash flood
would die of thirst
crossing these times

Adjusting to the Desert

It's been getting dark earlier
the light slipping away
before you notice winter
comes cruising up to the dock

You wonder as you watch
the light fade just how
that ship you've been expecting
can come in here where even
the memories of the sea
have long since dried up
and blown away   just then

Three stools down the moon
crosses her legs high
lights a cigarette and

Right at that moment
you know what it is
the coyotes keep askin' for

She leaves early after
driving everyone crazy
with the sound of her legs
drinking up their money
and making these promises
about how she'll show you
so much *more* tomorrow night

You listen to the broken
hearted cowboys *just so lonesome*
they could cry while outside
the stiff October wind tears
at the petals of a neon rose
spinning everything in sight
like some nervous kid
his first time on a bar stool

After closing you stand
on the ditchbank think
that by not expecting a great deal
or believing too strongly

In things that are either too much
or not enough here and counting

Only on the dizzy sense
of well being you get
under this totally
irrational sky

That *shit*
you just might get by

After all

I-80 Headed West

Comin' down out of the Sierra
everything that bright new
after a rain growth green
lady sittin' beside me
in the cab lookin' fine
legs up on the dash her
hand on my thigh beer
between my legs a joint
passin' round Merle Haggard
singin' *White Line Fever*
on the KRAK country corral
out the windshield
everything lookin good
just so god damned good

Piracy

Carpinteria

Full moon rising
comes in the open
window the sound
of a train high-ballin' it
through this small
lemon packing
town floats in the air
along with the smell
of *yesca* from a gold
metal flake Riviera
cruisin' this chick
on the street her
black slit skirt
flashin' all that
nylon leg tonight
on this the self
proclaimed safest
beach in the world
even the palms
are moving with
the sound of her
high heels on
the sidewalk
the howl of that
southbound freight

South Laguna

There must be something
to be said for all of this

All these blonds dressed
in some kind of hit me
with your best shot mentality

Talking from cocaine
Porsche to burgundy
Mercedes along the cliffs
as if the sun
were their very own

But at the moment

I'm damned if I know
what it could be

Snapshots

He sometimes noticed things
he was sure would take
a motor-drive Nikon
high-speed film to catch

But when he looked at them
later all he could see
was this old man snapping
a shot of hazy motionless ocean

And then quickly—as if afraid
of being caught yet somewhat
reverently satisfied as if
he'd just looked at a picture

Of someone he hadn't seen
in a long time—
slipping the Instamatic
into his hip pocket

Rounding Third
—for Harry Reese

He noticed it
walking home
from the store
a mushroom
cloud white
about the size
of a golf ball
he picked it
flipped it
in the air
two maybe three
times before
he caught
the glint
of the stream
over there
off to his left
and turned
and fired it
into the breeze
like a rising
second game
of the series
double that
takes off over
the center fielder's
head and he was
digging hard
for second
before he knew
for sure
it would go
and let up
floated
around third
watched it settle

into the creek
easily surely
as if slapping
the obligatory
after home run
hands still down
by one but feeling
good home safe
with two bags
of groceries
and a sixer

Listening to Hank Williams

In the bar she
tells him
she could

But it's not
what she
wants

In the store
she tells him
she can't
try on everything
or she won't
get anything

He pats a pint of booze
on his hip straightens
his John B. Stetson hat

She still
feels the glow
from that shot
back in the bar
balances on a pair
of wooden heels

While he digs
the bills
out of his coat
and pays

She slips
a black silk arm
through his

Under a barely turning
ceiling fan
they walk out
into a dusty neon night
with only a quarter
moon

For Now

She makes you up
a bed on the floor
of her all too frequently
otherwise occupied
gin and tonic eyes

And in lieu of pouring
time from hand to hand
you fluff the pillow
lie down

It doesn't really matter

It is enough

For now

Years later she

Or perhaps someone
who looks remarkably
like her will say

*Don't you want
to turn the light out
first*

And you trying
to weigh the cost
wanting to see
just what it is
will say

As you reach for her

*No, no
it doesn't matter
it's OK for now*

And it was

And it is

For now

Fractions

She's a painter
recently split
from her old man
also a painter
she tells me
of some note
who's sold out
found himself
a Santa Barbara
lady she speaks
of living fast
in the single lane
its drain
on her work
how it's better
with a relationship
that works
she wants me
to come by
the studio
look at her
paintings
especially
this big pink
one that is
somehow
very erotic
the canvases
are rectangular
divided
into grids
which
she fills
with sections
of circles
the titles
are fractions

seven
eighths
three quarters
nearly half

Things to Do at Jane's Cabin

Take a hike
up the creek
look at trees
as sculpture
check out
the deeper
pools but
don't see
any fish
split wood
find muscles
you'd forgotten
break a mixing
bowl wonder
where you'll
find another
catch up
with four
weeks of mail
lose interest
watch the pine
needles pile up
on the truck
wonder how she
got the place
be damn glad
she did find
what actually
appears to
be bear shit
in the woods

Piracy

Limping home from the office
like Wallace Beery's Long John
Silver he stopped at the store
was standing in the express
nine items or less waiting
to buy steak red wine cigarettes
when she walked up arms laden
with candy for the trick or treaters
low cut black blouse over
tight orange skirt black high heels
he saw himself in a cocktail party
room full of people where above
the collision of ice cubes the
muffled roar of conversation
he could hear that sudden swish
as she crossed her legs saw her
look up quickly wondering if
anyone had noticed that she
wished she wasn't standing
in line with these caramels
taffy and peppermints that
she wished she wasn't
buying all this stuff just
to sit home and give
away that maybe tonight
she could get all dressed up
go somewhere different
just for a night maybe see
from across a bourbon and
water filled room someone
watching her walk across
the parking lot like a pirate
skull and crossbones moon
rising quickly above the
neon motel rendezvous

Hindsight

The Photograph

It is probably somewhere
in the Pacific Northwest

The wallpaper appears damp
looks like it has been for years

Soft wet mildewed
the colors running
like someone's long
forgotten sheets

There is an old dresser
placed diagonally
across the corner
of the room

It is probably oak but
painted over badly
chipped four pedestals
the center area
covered with clean
white doilies

On each of the pedestals
there is a small jar
with some kind of flowers
that don't grow anywhere
around here in the front
right-hand corner
a kerosene lantern

There are probably other
objects in the room but
my eyes aren't as good
as they once were
I can no longer make them out

And it was taken so long ago
I cannot *remember* what they were

On the Dresser

Beginning to yellow and curl
stuck in the lower right
hand corner of a mirror
is the small snapshot
of an attractive young redhead
taken probably around 1946
in Southern California

She has posed herself
on the fender of a car
crossed her legs high
so you can see
the metallic sheen
of her black satin slip

It is a much deeper black
than the palm tree shadows
on a white stucco wall
behind the large silver
hoops which tug heavily
on her pierced ears

Mason Lake

Dull gray winter days

Water that penetrates
to the bone
infecting everything
with a dampness
that never dries

All day fussing
with firewood
so wet it does little
other than smoke
and sizzle

The neighbor's boat
has filled and sunk

My son goes out
to give the ducks
some bread

As he comes back in
I'm trying to dig
a coffee cup
out of the mountain
of unwashed dishes

The Franklin stove
sounds like a steam plant
outside even the ducks

Are beginning to complain

Something No One Catches

I know something
I'd like to tell you

But you don't want
to listen

Don't want to hear
what I have to say

Wait

Listen

Although the rain cleared
the sunset was troublesome
like never knowing what to say
to someone who asks
how you've been

It was as small distant
and red as the eyes
you pass in cattle trucks
on a late night highway
their breath steaming
into the air
through those little round holes

And

After it was gone

It was so still

I could hear
the fish jump clean
on the other side
of the lake

Exactly Eight Degrees

Six to eight small rounds
of maple that's been down
for *'bout a year* is s'posed
to be dry but still
smokes sizzles
when split and burned
in a Franklin stove
for seven hours say
from eight to three
on a rainy Saturday
will in the course
of that time raise
the temperature of
the house exactly
eight degrees

When It Will Happen

Sometime perhaps by accident
as if finding a forgotten note
hidden among your underwear

Sometime perhaps for no
apparent reason at all
while walking past
a store window admiring
your reflection or some
morning while putting
on your makeup

Sometime perhaps a long time
from now after I'm gone

It will happen

I am sure of it

You will think of me

The brief smile at the memory
of us will fall from your hand
as you burst into tears

And then as it shatters
right there in front of you
you'll realize
what you should have known

Finally see
what you should
have fucking seen

So very long ago

Edges

I

Sittin' in front of the fire
tryin' to stay warm
a lonesome cowboy
in my radio

Thinkin' about maybe
takin' a ride
all the way down
to where palm trees live

Watchin' it start
to get dark
the fog begin
to form out over
the lake

Wonderin' why
no matter how bright
the water doesn't
reflect the much
written about stars
above can't light
the dark below

Like a fool my radio
says

*to want to ride on a train
when the trains is all gone*

II

Socked in for four days
a pea soup one so thick
that the dock just twenty
feet outside my window
has shoved off
never to be seen again

But today
for a moment
just for a moment
a pale white sun
almost burned through

There was a minute
of blue sky
the lake tried to crawl
from an inky gray
toward green
the dock
was sighted
steaming toward shore

Then it came swirling
back nearby
things couldn't
hold their edges
grew soft went out
of focus began
to fade

Like the memory
of a totally pleasant day
from your own
not too distant
past

Rheumatoid Variants

You cannot move
from in front
of the stove
even forget
about chasing
the few winter
flies that have
made it in out
of the cold
from your brow

Your son tells you
it's important to know
where the flies go

You don't know
what happens to them

But like them
you are thankful
just to be able
to move around
is some kind
of minor miracle

A few new poems

And palm trees
on the glass
around your
three fingers
of rum

Hindsight

Greener pastures in time turn
to Indian summer brown
severe fire danger hills
which go up in smoke

And then
under constant driving rain
with nothing to hold it

Slide
right through your fingers

West

Nevada

Waltz

Mustard Colored Rain

Going back retracing your steps
looking for something you've lost

Something you had
at least thought you did
once

In the only theatre
of a small Nevada town
you watch film
begin to run
crazily back toward
its canister

It is old badly scratched
hard to see through
what appears to be
mustard colored rain

You cannot see
exactly what was going
on back there

But that's where you must have
lost something you need now

The keys that will unlock
your door heat
the early morning dark

So you squint
and keep on looking

The Misfits

Clark and Marilyn are sitting in a bar
in Reno drinking doubles talking
about leaving not to any place in
particular just moving on getting out

The jukebox is spouting something
about hanging in and hanging on
like autumn leaves before they fall

It was true it would be an early
winter for although there were few
trees in Reno to shed their leaves
the honkers were already heading
south and it was only the 23rd of August

They could barely hear the music
above the dull mechanical roar
of the casino—a combination
of dollars dropped into slots
handles being pulled and bells
going off every time someone
put in three and got two back

There were old women sitting on red
naugahyde stools pulling the handles
again and again with a slow desperate
assembly line familiarity as if
they had sat on those same stools
for twenty-five years

You know she says *I walked out*
to the city limits once, it didn't
look like much was out there

Clark kills his drink in one gulp
motions to the bartender to bring
them another round nods at her
and says *Yeah, but it may be the*
only place there's anything left

They look at one another across
the table and something passes
between them like a sudden breeze
across the furnace of a Nevada afternoon

They leave the bar find his
battered pickup drive up Virginia
to 4th Street and then head east
into the desert leaving Reno
and a technicolor even in
black and white sunset
behind them

Looking at Maps

The Great Basin least spectacular
of all North American deserts
almost the entire state contained
within its boundaries

Where what would barely pass
elsewhere for a stream
is a river and none of them
will ever find the sea

Even so we have less water
and more desert around us
than anywhere else
including Arizona

The county has had more than 70
towns come but because the ore
played out fired burned them out
or the water dried up only Fallon
continued to grow

Today the eastern county line
is not known exactly the western
edge of town reaches toward Reno
saying Raley's   Sprouse Rietz
Country Kitchen   Kentucky Fried Chicken

But if you look at the old maps
and listen

You hear

Bango   *Bell Flat*
Bolivia   *Bunejug Mountains*

Carson Sink   *Cocoon Mountains*
Dixie Valley   *Dead Camel Mountains*

Eastgate   *Eightmile Flat*
Forty Mile Desert   *Frenchman's*

Hard To Find Mine   Hazen
Ione   Job's Peak

La Plata   Middlegate
Mirage   Mopung Hills

Quicksilver Mine   Ragtown
Salt Wells   Sand Mountain

Seeho Springs   Stillwater
Stinking Springs   Swingle Bench

Westgate   White House Rock
Wildcat Station   Wonder

Yomba

Finding Stillwater

It's really not that hard
to find although many
have passed by few stopped
fewer yet stayed

Not even the county seat
remained for long

It's not that everything
you need will be here
it's that so much you don't
will *not* be

So bring what you cannot
give up wanting
with you think of it
as a place you're always
it seems either coming
from or going to

It's not that far
from where you are
right now calling
probably from
a bar uptown

And although it sometimes
looks out the window
an awfully lot like
it feels inside your head
before you adjust your
margins put the paper in

Right now there are clouds
the color of the light
in the center of a glass
of white wine floating
around on the faded
blue Levi's of the sky

Mirage Factor

There are several things about
the weather around here that
you can more or less count on
among them heat cold and wind

It's rare to draw three
at once but a pair
is not unusual

Adding to the wind you
draw one of those winter come
back in late March days

On which you have to go
into Reno on *business*

And it's somewhere around Mustang
or Painted Rock where it's gusting
at seventy or eighty miles an hour
there's an eighteen-wheeler jack
knifed on the interstate and

The car heater going full tilt
can't hold off the cold

That you realize that you've
been here *right here*
before the feeling strikes
suddenly as they say
without warning

You see coming home
through the dust and tumbleweeds
the inverted reflections
of distant things grow closer

Last fall's leaves are sucked up
to float around and around
in front of you

And then although lightning's

not supposed to twice
you watch the sun
in your rearview mirror
drop into what you
distinctly remember as

The humming mosquito colored air
of a late last July afternoon

Ten Gallon Clouds

It's after midnight

For the first time
since seven this morning
you switch the cooler off

Just five minutes ago
you're sweating already

What was left of the moon
finally came up

Too hot to sleep you turn on
the one channel you get
out here in the desert
John Wayne's lawless frontier
is all there is

110 today

Hotter tomorrow
the forecast
calls for *some* clouds

In the afternoon you'll
probably even wish for rain
just to cool things down
but you know it will not come
know that you'll
have to wait it out

As the ichthyosaurs must have

Drying up with the sea

Here
where the dark and light
collide

Under the blankets of the sky

Reflections in a Desert Wind

The mirror is chipped pitted
its surface almost worn away
from the constant battering
of driven sand

The images look as if they
have been there a long time but
appear suddenly like middle age

The onset of arthritis at 32
a desert wind on a 99° day
you can actually see it moving
toward you

At first it doesn't look like
it will be *that* bad the climate
after all is supposed
to be good for it

Then you see from 70 miles away
a twelve-foot woman on fire
a man on trial for shooting
his four-month-old son

Finally its strength is too much
the saplings have all bent double
everything is layered with fine dust

You watch the tumbleweeds let go
roll with the rippling metal sound
mobile homes make on such a day
and for a while you're moving along
fairly well but any sudden intrusion
or marshaling of the facts
even small ones stretched thin
taut as wire between fenceposts
hangs you up stops you are stuck
there so long even the smallest
amount of effort becomes too much

Though you can still hear it
coming from some distance off
like the by now only half-remembered
song of her wind blown hair
moving across the desert's face

So you listen but no longer know
if this is the right place
or if like holding a door
or a coat it's just
a matter of being there
at the right time

Look

Even the curtains are dancing
straight out in the air almost
parallel to the floor

Distance

Moving away

It takes a while for things
you thought lost to reappear
but sooner or later they do
and you find the differences
are not ones of contrast
but the lack of it

Gone are the salt white clouds
and deep azure sky *there*
things were more diffuse
less certain a TV set with
no contrast everything
was gray muted

Once you left the desert's heat
to sit in front of a wood stove
most of the day trying to decide
which was the right piece
to burn next which would catch
and not fill the house with smoke

While through your window you watched
greens and blues even the blacks
of a moonless night bleed into gray
under the constant billowing rain

After five straight days it
finally let up and became
so foggy that even though
the softest sounds were amplified
they remained as distant
as the worn out feelings
of an old record

Fallon

You've driven over
nine hundred miles
just to be here
for a few days
where it's warm
enough
dry enough
to sit on the porch
in the sun on the day
after Christmas
under a sky
you'd almost forgotten
could be so blue

The few clouds
are so high and thin
that when they pass
in front of the sun
there's no change
in the light and
it takes a while
for you to feel
your shirt growing
cold against your skin

But the chill
passes quickly
like a first snow
that sticks around
only in the shadows
of the ditchbank

So you decide
to walk up
get the mail
with the sky
the only coat
around you

Seeing the Light

Warm

Under that late afternoon
mid-February bright blue sky

With salsa in the kitchen
window full of immense blue
backed flat bottomed white clouds
floating by honky tonks and
harsh lights on your radio

The air is as crisp
as the light

You can see it coming
for miles and miles

Sneaking in and out
of the clouds as if
looking for someplace
better safer
to stash the loot

And finding no place better

Than right here

West Nevada Waltz

*I learned how to listen
for a sound like the sun going down*
—RODNEY CROWELL

It isn't so much a matter
of not looking a gift horse
in the mouth but rather
a matter of not looking
any horse in the mouth

Out here valleys are measured
in miles *across* and no matter
how long it takes out there
in the middle
under the sun
you like fall always
seem to arrive
just barely in time

After a while there's no longer
enough left to waste
on crossing the damn things
just to see if it's any better
over there after all
are folks who've pretty
much decided the same thing

Somewhere along the line
even though there are those times
when like a horse tethered in one place
too long you reach the end of your rope
you begin to settle in

Begin to forget the *orange cherry
orange* combinations which didn't
pay off and noticing only how easily
the bright yellow leaves all around
this so-called oasis let go start
to waltz toward the ground

you believing she just might
show up again

Begin to wait for the moon

Which like an expected check
always takes too long shows
up late stumbling
across the black ice of the sky
like a tipsy redhead in high heels
full but still in the 1981s
only worth a quarter

She's not much what with her makeup
smeared all too often looking the next
day like noontime neon—showing only
a hint of what she was the night before

But right now up there shimmering
almost dancing across that nimble
three-quarter-time blue sky she
looks like the damndest schooner
you ever did see and of course

There are the clouds

Painting

Coffee

He put the water on
sat with country roads
on the radio the pieces
of his busted-up guitar

Trying to figure
or at least remember
trying to make a cup
some sense out of something

This would be cowboy
wasn't movin'
like he used to
kept stumblin' over
what he should be
steppin' on

He stood at the window
thinking about how nice
it might be—
someone to rub his back

He watched the wind
swirl the dusty bourbon air
heard that slap
of the wooden screen door

Times here weren't so good
but really not so bad
either

He ground his own beans
drank it black

Moments

You sit there
try to remember
when *that* was
just how long ago

You saw yourself
in this or that
sepia yellowed
snapshot memory

Standing there
holding nothing
as if it were a fish

The Color of Water

—for Jess

Around here the wind rolls
with no particular destination

Moves like a knife
toward its target

Until
exhausted by the attempt

It stretches out
tries to hold onto
the color of water

Which is of course
the color of those naked trees
madly waving in answer
to questions yet to be asked

How It Is

It is colder
than anyone
around here
can remember
it ever getting

Rain turns to snow
covers the alkali
and salt grass
for two weeks
the usually bluer
than anyplace else
sky is the color
of a daytime moon
a neon wind
pulls the color
from everything
even the sage

Then it clears off
temperatures *really*
drop pipes freeze
tree limbs snap
break you buy
another kerosene
heater close off
rooms scrape
ice from the inside
of your kitchen windows

You wait
for better days
read old poems
know that
you are no longer
young enough
to be coy about it

Things really
weren't
any better
back then
back *there*

But there were a few
bright moments poems
caught here and there
like dew in a web

Finally it begins
to thaw

Things come back
things you've
forgotten
come popping up
through the snow
even the moon
is back
in the black

The snow's melting
off you're drunk
on the coming
through the window
sun hitting your back
and haven't yet realized
that tomorrow
will be nothing
but mud

It is like love

Which more
than anything else is
those few bright moments
in between

Waiting for the Call

How can you explain
what 3:30 will bring

I know it will probably
be late but

Try and be as precise
as you can

Where will the hands be
what will they be doing

Holding a brush
a book of poems

Or grasping at straws
It's hard to tell

Tentative as they are
not wanting to put

That final one
on the camel's back

Water

Looks good
on the surface cool
if you're hot still
moving if you're
frozen stiff

But go below
that carefully polished
ready to present
to the public surface
and it gets messy
slippery hard
to hang onto
the dark secrets
of hidden boulders

Spots so deep
all light
all sense of direction
even the ability to move
is lost

You realize it too late

Try to call out
above the roar
of receding clouds

Dancing around
and finally down
the great blue basin
of the sky

Tahoe

Out on the deck
astride a certain point
of the afternoon

There is not much
noise

An occasional voice
drifts up from the lake
the sotto voce
of Chopin's piano

Clouds boil over
the ridge to the west
stretch thin white talons
toward my chardonnay
and something

Perhaps the sky's envy
of *that* blue
causes the wind
to begin to move slowly

At first

The notes from a flute
begin to lift

The edges of the water

All Day Long

The air has been choked
thick with yellow dust
swirling like some angry
top around the basin

Finally late
in the afternoon
the clogged faucet clears
the rain begins and

It looks as if it's hailing
the manic yellow ochre
of a Van Gogh peeling
there in the afternoon

In between cloudbursts
sun struck wheatfield

Punctuation

Lust colored hair that when
properly punctuated by rain
wrestling in the liquid air
sounds as if it could be
mighty fine indeed
to be tangled there

Gray

Rain for a week
he left no note

He'd been seen
walking
by the river
thirty minutes
before

But it probably
looked too cold
and he retreated
back into
a short dog
of white port

Then climbed
six flights
of stairs
after not
being able
to quite figure
out the elevator

Walked once
around the rim

Where he could not
equal as it may have been

Find
even the smallest
patch of blue

One Deep Breath

Deceptive as the sun
breaking through fifteen
ice every morning till noon
days—beautiful for a while
but soon growing dreary
two pots of coffee by ten
watching for that package
the one that should arrive
today and with one deep
breath illuminate a landscape
the luminists would have loved

A Body of Work

He started counting

He did not know
exactly
where to begin

But he began
keeping this
discarding that
counting only
the former

Later
some of the latter
became as attractive
as a diamond
shaped sign looming
suddenly up out of the fog

Just in time
to lean into the curve
without breaking the thought
he was trying so hard
to hang onto

Delivering the Show

Frain across the state
for nine days no one
in the valleys has seen
the sun and those
who've left only when
they hit the summit

Where briefly
the landscape
is equal parts Nepal
and Diebenkorn before
slipping back down
into sixty miles
of tule fog

Approaching Valmy

The song
your threadbare
tires sing
to the asphalt
at three A.M.
just fourteen
miles out of
Valmy Nevada
with now even
the Great Salt Lake
airborne and
drifting off
into the rearview

Battle Mountain

Valley fog lifts
only over the pass

Air so heavy
in the Owl Club

I could not stay

Tonopah

Sunday twenty degrees
she's buying a twelve pack
digging in her parka for change
rocking back and forth
in red pumps chattering
on and on and on
about how it could be
worse how it could be
for Christ's sake
Butte

November 2nd

The light has changed
crystallized into cold
bands of hazy yet intense
color

The mountains to the east
glow like stubborn wood
hanging onto what is left
of the light

Huddled around the embers
of a dark line
drawn by the night
two days into November

Gossip

The wind is whispering
among last month's
stripped clean branches

Trying to stir something up
pushing fallen leaves
across the sand

Swirling here and there
into the blunt semaphore
of a wavering twilight

Spreading a small
naphthol smudge
across the lip of the sky

Getting Across

the signs say KEEP MOVING
—RICHARD SHELTON

After leaving the confused
footsteps of a neon twilight
behind

And driving out here you begin
taking it apart watching piece
by high gloss enamel piece
fade and peel in the desert sun
until a fine white powder falls
from tubes that can no longer
remember the hum and buzz of color

You look at everything closely
shift it slightly as if hoping
that sudden play of light
will lend it more than
it has to offer

The words you thought so right
have begun to sound like sand
in the margins of a place
no one dares to cross
and everywhere around the edges
are shards of broken amber glass

Saying *you are not the first*
to think about trying it here

Thirty-Seven

Outside the wind is busy
sanding everything down
to only what must remain

And with chapped senseless
lips stands there muttering
of what it could have been

Painting

I feel as if I am too near the sky
all the time
    —MARSDEN HARTLEY

The mountains appeared
to be right there
at the end of this road
but he knew
they were close to
maybe a hundred miles off

He was sitting on the lawn
thinking about a figure ground
relationship that would
hold together work even
when looked at closely
for a long time

Sooner or later he
like the leaves would know
it was time and when he did
as much from necessity
as choice
he'd have to go

Have to move again
like clouds just can't
keep still changing
from one thing to another
right before his eyes

The cool September afternoon
grass of his childhood
where he watched biplanes
form letters overhead
began to itch and
the skywriting came apart

With a horrible cracking sound
that ended up hanging there

for years like some bad motel
room painting just above
his line of vision

It was a landscape
into which winter came
sooner than expected

Outside trees with half
their leaves still on
broke under the strain

The birds he thought he had
in his hands pulled together
into a raggedy pink flock
and headed south the brief
purple orange rush of joy
on the mountains
gradually turning gray

Before it was gone

Driving

to

Vegas

Waiting

For an answer to your letter
the pitcher to make his move
toward the plate
the proofs to come back
from the printer

Waiting in lines
banks grocery stores
the post office

Waiting out the rain
for the sun to go down
for the moon to come up

For the paint to dry

Waiting

For the leaves to fall
the fever to break
for the check to arrive
your lover your wife to turn
toward you with a smile

Waiting

Waiting for the wind
to lift a skirt

For the world to wake up
and notice

Driving

Sometimes
if I can find it
I look at the map

How far it is
from here to there

We're all different
tend to end up
I suppose
where it's best

But still we yearn
to get from here
to there

Others who are impatient
with all this distance
make these roads bright

Brake lights strung along
the cloudless interstate
Great Basin night

Four or Five Beers
Dorsey's Bar
Gabbs, Nevada

Don't know why
I came out here

Circumstances
I guess

Weren't no woman
or the law

Probably
just 'cuz the wheel
didn't turn right

And you know
I've left
more'n a few times

But after a while
I start to feel like ice
must as it freezes
and I end up comin' back

You know
I can't complain
if I get rained on

I know
it ain't no picture show

Outside Ely in the Rain

Bleary-eyed four A.M. cafe
your breath floating
in front of you

Suddenly catches
the sound of a fan
back and forth

Back and forth

The crackles of red neon
push through the rain
across a damp gray field

Stinking of sage

Not Quite Dark

And still over eighty

Driving home
the twenty watt bulbs
of bathrooms adrift
in alfalfa begin
to throw their rays
of hope up into
the leaving indigo
turning oh so quickly
to mars black sky
which now appears
to be running
right alongside
the car

Your hand's out
the window
knitting feeble
white dots together
as it floats along
feeling the air
squeeze its flesh
like some not
quite ready
avocado

Sifting

Wood screws
loose
in a drawer

Too many
different
sizes

No two
alike

All too
short
to hold it
together

All of them

For one reason
or another

Somehow
worth saving

It's Not As If Everything Came from New York

It's as if we're crossing this river
on foot the current stronger
than we thought

We step cautiously into still spots
tell ourselves to think about depth
think instead about getting burned

While we are swept away

Schwitters

Hearing the rain break up in syllables
—PAMELA STEWART

Early but never early enough
I come to shave the idea
of my face in the morning mirror

If only I knew where
everything is supposed to be
that is impossible

But something is near
and I can hear the rain
breaking up in syllables

Speaking slowly
trying out a new tongue
one nearly as fluid

As when love is new and
things fall together like
scraps in a Schwitters collage

Of crumpled blue sky
I keep looking
out the window

Wondering just where
you are right now
nothing is as innocent

Or as unconnected
as we once
so naively thought

In the cabinet
six separate bottles
all saying *pain*

Seurat

The disappearance of days
accelerated came to be measured
solely by the mail the day the date

Being replaced by *this year*
beginning amid the drone
of last year's bloated promises

Cast ashore thrown so far
above high tide line
the cartridges are jammed

Into the chambers and spun
like shattered fragments of the sky
into a bitterly pointillistic notion

That it was all probably due
to things best not spoken of
no not here

Neon

She's short
dark but
looks pale

In the almost
purple
motel light

Talks about
possibilities
about dancing

A two-step
across the wreck
of the West

He begins
to think
twice

The same
thought

Blinking
on and off

Above
the cars
huddled
in a desperate lot

Pollock

Look closely you'll begin to see
the splattered chrome bumper
reflections of a turquoise
'59 El Camino in the parking lot
slick with rain

The smell of wet asphalt
her fugitive scent
black leather red hair
nothing, nothing at all under
those madly waving colors

Rothko

Hanging on here
is it
that way there
too

The early March
afternoon clock
ticking one
more one less

Pacing
back and forth
if you want
you can

Perhaps change
you don't think
that's enough
but look

The smoke
from my cigarette
always rises
takes your eyes

Away from the ice
as it melts
in your glass
trapped here

Under the lust
and closed air
of a compressed
Rothko sky

Hopper

An off white tempera afternoon
in a would be chrome diner

The sun attempts
to pour meaning
into what is best
seen at closing time:

Last night
the slit ebony
cloth of the sky
revealed the cross
legged flesh of the moon

High heels hooked
on the rung of a stool
hanging on
in the trembling bar sign light

Arts Administration

In the bar
we wonder
why
we bother
to continue
the trying
to find
a place
for the artist
ending up
taking
all of Art's
time

Twilight in San Juan

Hornitos blue jeans and neon
back of the bar reminded him
of the sound of her heels
moving down the hallway
of that cheap hotel in San Juan
stopping in front of 214
to retrieve something
that tumbled out of her
hastily packed bag she lit
a cigarette before moving
on down the cadmium splashed
walls without once looking back

RNO–LAX

Over an hour late
fog at SFO is the excuse
for another drink
after lunch with Heizer
scale is the issue
time the question
distance the difference
if you're on the left
you've got a nice view
of the city on the right
the unspeakable blackness
of the Pacific
flight attendant makes
last pass for glasses
small bells in her ears
and hard eyes I remember
the color of her stockings
the same as Michael's
earth colored cement
and the less than half
dollar sized moon
dropping off to the left
as we descend into a sea
of lights that punishes
the limits of our vision

Fog at the Borders of the Palms

The discordant music of the twentieth century
is small recompense for a mist
that thickens the air conducts
the wind and a light so horrible
that it could never note any music
nor guide us through the daily accident
as we lean into each other in an unmade room

Drawing to an Inside Straight

Dust swirls behind you
down Indian Lakes Road

Almost there
you tell yourself

No longer sure why
you're going what
will happen

When you get there
fish and white pelicans

Do you remember the time
your son slipped under
gagging spitting
as he broke the surface
glad to see the sky

The time you came
on a picnic

Today there's nothing
only what the wind
left behind

Muttering
in the trees

Yeah, yeah
shut up and deal

Driving to Vegas

Tonopah's
the place
contour lines
appear
to rise

Between there
and Goldfield
the first
Joshua trees

Beer at the Mozart Club

From then on
it's all downhill

Between Mercury
and Indian Springs
the light
begins to change

You wonder
what you'll do
when you reach
the edge
of the map

Out there
on the horizon

All that neon

Beckoning you

In from the dark

Red

Web

The Opening

Every year or so
whatever it is
you've been trying
to figure out

At whatever point
it's gotten to

Is packed up carted off
hung somewhere
for a month
maybe six weeks

That first night people
you've never seen
maybe met once
somewhere show up

Briefly it's nice
watching the social swirl
in front of your work

Cheap white wine for anyone
who holds out
their plastic cup three hours
it's all over except
for the lame reviews
in Sunday's paper

Which will miss the point
if not totally

Then at least completely

Fishin' in the Dark
—for Michael Sarich

I

Wonder why
I think too much
expanding explodes
what I just
convinced myself
was there

To think I can
be strong
or over matter
is bullshit

Attempting meaning
thinking
makes me thirsty
I try to forget
all I've over
estimated

Don't really know
who I am
what I'm supposed to be
which one
is me
under this carefully
polished surface

Try and hold on
to what I see
but everywhere I look
sideways and around
honesty is dissolving
before it reaches
the edge

I'd much rather
float around safe
up here
in senseless blue

II

Juggling
what's good
what's bad

Why
we always get
hit here

A closely stoppered vial
rattling around
in an open and shut case

It's always too close

Then too far

Touch and fear
striped open hungry
mouths on a barber pole

Juggling

What's good
what's bad

Why we always
get hit

Here

III

Touch fear pain

Seem to make things
real if you can
touch them

If you can
if it goes
this far
if you can
feel it

It's real

The senseless mumblings
of pure touch

IV

The real heart the real
head

Has to take it
from the other two

Has to feel it
when

They open they close
their god damn fish tail hands
trying
to hold me in place

Still it comes
to the surface

If you feel it

It's true

V

Touch fear pain

Seem to make things
real if you can
touch them

If you can if it goes
this far
if you can
feel it

It's real

The senseless mumblings
of pure touch

VI

Don't care what
they all say

I hear more
than you think

It ends up here
where things
really
get polished

After all that
philosophical moaning
it's simply
biological

After all

It's what I'm supposed to do

Greatness and stupidity
wrapped up in one

Artists' Statements

Aesthetics is for artists like ornithology is for birds. An object never serves the same function as its image or its name. Take an object. Do something to it. Do something else to it. Do something else to it. I only know my materials, to what end I know not. It doesn't have anything to do with materials, or style . . . it's a kind of energy that comes into the particular sequence of events. Art is a marriage of the conscious and the unconscious. Art disease is caused by a hardening of the categories. It's more important to be in the theatre than it is to know what's going on in the movie. Living in the desert has taught me to go inside myself for shade. Without music life would be a mistake. A writer is not so much someone who has something to say as he is someone who has found a process that will bring about new things he would not have thought of if he had not started to say them. I have nothing to say and I am saying it and that is poetry. Poetry is always a dying language but never a dead language. The grass is always greener on the other side of the fence, but it's just as hard to cut . . . few understand how past and over the past is. Language (or the absence of it) is extremely critical for the conceptualization of imagery. When critics get together they talk about form and space. When painters get together they talk about turpentine. Talking about art is like trying to French kiss over the telephone.

Barnett Newman. Rene Magritte. Jasper Johns. Kurt Schwitters. William T. Wiley. Jean Cocteau. Ad Reinhardt. David Byrne. Richard Shelton. Frederich Nietzsche. William Stafford. John Cage. Robert Smithson. Little Richard. Donald Kuspit. Pablo Picasso. Terry Allen.

Personal Values, 1952

It was mid-afternoon, he was still out in the studio, painting. She lit some candles, took a hot bath and lingered, drinking cognac, until the water cooled. She shaved her legs, got out of the tub and sat on the hamper. She pulled on her stockings, enjoying the feel of the silk on her legs as she walked into the bedroom, pausing to pull back and tie the white lace curtains.

Outside, the fluffy white clouds skidded around the corners of the sky. She decided on the black dress, *quelle suprise,* the one he'd bought her in Brussels, and a black pearl choker. It probably didn't matter, what he always noticed first was her legs, and her shoes. He'd even done a painting, a very sexy painting, of them. He had been the only one to pay attention to how she dressed. She kind of liked that. And she loved his mind, how he infused everything, even watching her eat raspberries and ice cream, with some kind of symbolic resonance.

She was supposed to meet him at 5:30 but didn't feel like going. She wasn't sure why. Recent events and the objects associated with them seemed to have grown larger, seemed to be occupying much more of her thoughts than she'd like.

She decided that she really wasn't feeling that well after all. Perhaps lunch had been a bit too spicy. She was suddenly very tired but decided against lying down—she felt exposed, as if she was outdoors, half-naked, on a windy day. Besides the bed looked entirely too small to be comfortable.

To get ready she had to dig through the wardrobe, try and find the dress and decide on which shoes. When she passed the wardrobe, she liked what she saw in the mirror. She had redded her hair, and although right now the thought of having to comb the snarls out of it was unbearable, she knew it would all be worth it.

4:37 A.M.

Just the smell
hay under
a quarter moon
pushes toward you

Just the clouds
in early light
that try
to mimic her hair

Just an empty
hangar crickets
keep calling for

Just the leaves
calling you
to the door

Just watching
darkness give up
more than you thought
possible

But look
the sun has begun
to crawl over
the Stillwaters

And now
rim to rim
the sky is streaked
with red tendrils

Moving

Moving in your mind

Driving to Montana with V.

—for Bill Kittredge

Anaconda Gillette Goldfield
Havre Sheridan Winnemucca
so many others

Seems you always
come in against the wind
with just the right light
inside which you hear
the ripple of trailer tops
squatting on the edge of town

Most have given up all hope
of ever seeing rubber again
jealous of so-called mobile homes
that have never seen it

A little farther in
sheet-metal shop buildings
have tried to settle
only to become flaking
in the sun WWII Quonset huts

Closer to the center
western stores
red brick neon bars
the *places* of those
that tried it here first

All of them

All of them
trying to remember
over five or six beers
in the center of a hazy valley floor

What they felt like
the first time they saw
those mountain peaks
break a windy aluminum colored sky

Out Here

—for D. R. Wagner

On the antennae
of what we feel

My hands
on this page

Only

To feel you
on the other side

Of these words

Howling

You hear the sound
for miles and miles wind
howling from the heart
when it feels
passion's deposition
being taken elsewhere

Looking

Someone with your hair
didn't have your eyes

Someone with your eyes
didn't have your smile

Someone with your smile
didn't have your legs

Someone with your legs
didn't have your spirit

Someone with your spirit
didn't have my heart

It's been out
driving all night long

Across the desert's face
looking

Looking

Looking for you

Poetics

What you can get
somebody to believe
they haven't
thought of before

At Workman's

Spring almost
Easter

Walking amidst
brightly growing things

Offers solace
from the days

Reminds me
of last year

Your words
then as now

Stargazer lilies whisper
love without clocks

Overwintered bleeding hearts
speak of having dinner

By the flickering candlelight
of how it's getting better

Driving God & the Grieving Widow

It starts out with who
done what to who

Soon becomes
Lit-Crit

Poetry and the Novel
having a family dispute

The canine novelist
peeing on everything in sight

While the feline poet
sneaks next door

Eats the neighbor's food

Metaphor

—for David Lee

Gawd I don't know
what the fuck this is

But

Gimme that

Gawd damn hammer

And I'll hit it

Exquisite

Beautiful

As in her
big mouthed
high heeled grin
purposefully striding
across the room

Also

Intense

As in

Bone pain

Heartbreak

Candle

Clouds sliding over
the Sierra as he came
around the bend
reminded him

A black pleated skirt
her grin under
hooded eyes
swinging her legs
high into the truck

Her hand on the back
of his neck the unexpected
candle suddenly lit

Dust

Coalesces
in the autumn air

Wraps me
in her hand

Like rain on October fields
Austin to San Antonio

Her skin pale
as love's first
evening star

In a room
high above
the Rio Colorado

Fado for a Sultry Afternoon
With the Blinds Partly Pulled

They are in an oceanside motel, just across the tracks
from the beach. It is a hot, sultry afternoon. There
is the red splash of a Bougainvillea, limp from
the heat, trailing over the balcony railing. The
palm trees are motionless. Even the ocean seems
too tired to make waves of any sort. The blinds are
partly pulled and a shaft of late afternoon sunlight
has found its way across the room to her blazing auburn
hair. "What're you thinking?" she asks. He'd been
sitting there thinking, trying to come up with a title
for a book of poems. Nothing was coming. "Oh,
nothing," he replies, sets his glass down and looks
up. She has on a short, black silk dress and is
straightening her stockings. She walks toward him,
her heels clicking across the tile floor, her dress
rustling in the pellucid air. She perches on the edge
of a chair, crosses her legs and sips on the Campari
and soda. She looks very, very good. "Don't
worry about it, baby," she says, "It'll come."

Red Web

Mid-afternoon
she sleeps in
the intricate web
of her hair
holding the pillow
in place

He had the sweet
taste of her
in his mustache
was listening

To the sound
of the breeze
in a bottlebrush

The sigh of his heart
mourning doves
in the trees

A little farther out
the muffled roar
of the 405

Six or seven lanes
of metal boxes
in each direction

Rushing toward
the death of their dreams

Desert

Saudade

Music

—for Valerie & for Jack Fulton

Dave saved up his money and bought a bar. He liked
classical music and since the bar was in the middle of the
Great Basin night miles from the likelihood to hear any
such thing, he decided what the hell, called it the Mozart
Club. He really couldn't remember whether it was
Chopin, Satie, Mozart, or Mendelssohn that had moved
him so, but he liked the sound of Mozart. He painted a
big skeleton on the side of the bar emblazoned with the
legend, "This Guy Drank Water." A lot of local folks
thought that was pretty funny and began to call the
watering hole home.

Every month or so Dave and this painter friend of his
would make the day-long drive to Reno on a supply run.
They were at the Santa Fe and had consumed way too
many picons and that great Friday night Basque steak
dinner. They were standing around the bar drinking
Winnemucca coffees, debating whether they should head
back or not and if they did who, given all the picons, was
the most qualified to drive, when she walked in.

She was the most drop-dead beautiful woman you'd ever
seen. She could have been Northern Italian or English or
Irish, what with that stunning mane of red hair and those
amazing legs. But she was, in fact, Austrian. After a quick
look around she walked to the end of the bar and sat on
a stool, crossing her legs high. Dave, and everyone else in
the bar, was speechless. She had silenced that rowdy
Friday night crowd just by walking in like the way,
sometimes, the sun going down can stop a wind that's
been howling all day across the desert's face.

Dave watched his heart tumble out of his chest and flop
around on the bar like some fish sensing that it was, after
all, the seventh year of a drought and this just might be it.

"Would you like a drink?" he suddenly blurted out.

Their eyes locked and that was it. They spent the next three hours drinking at a small table in the back. Dave kept feeding her small slices of lime from the palm of his hand and she'd laugh, oh how she'd laugh. She'd get up every so often to go and call someone and Dave would watch her walk to the phone and back wondering, wondering . . . He even reached under the table once and squeezed her leg, thinking, oh my God what a stupid thing to do, now she'll walk out and I'll never see her again.

But she stayed and talked and drank and they both felt some kind of furnace burning within them like never before until, finally, she said, "I have to go. My brother's coming to pick me up."

She left with her brother. Dave left with his painter friend and they all ended up standing in the parking lot, Dave and her just staring at each other, neither wanting to break the connection. "Jeezus Christ, Dave," the painter said, "Put your god damn eyes back in your head and open the god damn door."

Who's to say what happened next or how it happened but Dave hung around until he saw her again and that's all it took. A done deal. Never a question. She came back to the Mozart Club with him. That's when the music really began. And from then on everyone kept commenting on how amazing it all was, how right it all seemed, how good they looked together, how glad they were for Dave.

This is it, Dave thought. At last. And he began of think of waltzing toward the millennium on a sea of melodious light. But then there's always life. It goes on, as they say. And it does. But it also can just suddenly stop. He went down to the bar one day and came home to find her gone. No note. No word. Nothing. Her clothes, her shoes— she was obsessive about her collection of black high heels —everything but her, still there. Dave looked and looked, went back up to Reno, but nothing. Not a trace. No one even knew her.

It was as if she had never existed, as if it had all never happened. But Dave knew it had and he tried to forget but couldn't because he didn't really want to forget. He never did look at another woman and he drank more than a bit and it was worse than fightin' the weather, all that thinking about it, wondering what had happened, why there were all these years of nights they might have been together, but weren't.

It was thirty years later, almost to the day, that this gorgeous redhead walked into the Mozart Club. Everyone was stumblin' over themselves, hittin' on her, trying to buy her a drink, everyone that is but Dave, who just sat at the end of the bar nursing his drink. But she wasn't interested in all the attention and only wanted one thing.

"Is there anyone here named Dave?" she asked.

"Down there, end of the bar," Dave's painter friend said.

She walked down to the end of the bar, everyone watching every part of her move. "Dave?" she asked.

"Yeah?" he said looking up from his drink, his bloodshot blues meeting her amber ones, "Whattya want?"

"I'm your daughter," she said.

And so the story was told. How her mother was from a very wealthy Austrian family; how she had come to the States on vacation with her brother; how she had walked into a bar in Reno one Friday night and fallen head-over-heels in love with the piercing blue eyes of a guy named Dave who owned a bar; how her grandmother had disowned her mother for having the audacity to do that; how after that it didn't seem to matter until her grandmother fell ill and wanted her daughter back home before she died; how her grandmother sent her son back to the States to kidnap her daughter; how her mother was in a car accident and they were able to save the baby, but not her; how her grandmother recovered, raised her and never mentioned any of it; how her uncle told her all about it only after her grandmother finally died.

Sierra Wind

Who could have known
that it would whip

Your hair to a frenzy
provoking fantasies

Of what it might
be like to be

Tangled there
heat from your eyes

Shimmering toward me
across the parking lot

What happened there
afterwards

I never felt the same
not ever

Not

Ever again

Rimbaud Stops at the Liquor Store in Mojave

The wind with so little
to hold its interest

Is making speeches
about her hair

The sky's full
of stained cotton fleece

The sound of drunken boats
filling the air

And nothing
nothing made much sense

Without her

Talkin' Cow-Calf Pairs at the Coney Island Bar

The bigger the hat

The smaller the ranch

January

Could be Butte Battle Mountain
Livingston or Lamoille

It's all about the same

In late January
rust pitted pickups
bounce around
3:00 A.M. chuckholes

Passenger doors
swinging open wide

Honey, I'm sorry
would you please
just get back
in the truck

Traffic

The longer you last, the less you care
— MARILYN MONROE

Why is it always late Friday
afternoon with one of the four
wheels of your heart going flat

That you find
someone behind you
wants to run up your ass

While up front someone
is braking in anticipation
of *it* actually breaking

Dilemma

The mistake always
trying to word it
too soon

The regret always
in not having
done it sooner

Thinking About You, Reading Creeley

Three hundred miles into
the midst of a Great Basin night

February thoughts of your red lips
tumble through my mind

Errors accumulate like late snow
in a high desert ditchbank

Building out of our sight
the terrible thoughts of time

What did I know thinking myself
able to go alone all the way

The Ole Mind-Body Split Healed

She thinks about swaying to Joe Ely
he thinks Leonard Cohen's lyrics
when she suddenly turns to him
asks about the words to *Suzanne*

Again and Again

I've been thinking
'bout nothing but you

For two straight days
your voice

The memory the fire
of your touch

Becoming liquid
sounds the scroop
of your skirt

As you descend
the staircase take
me in your mouth

Becoming the liquid
line drawn by my tongue
through your delta

Sounds
so much like music

Sliding into you
that even the rain
bursts into flame

Gardening

January quickly becomes July
around here what you plants

Comes in spades

Or not at all

The Perennial's Lament

Spring fully sprung
again

I find myself
talking

To this year's leaves
about

Exactly the same
things

I spoke of

To last year's

Independence Day

Standing by the fence
listening to low-down blues

Fireworks over Rattlesnake pale
fade in comparison

To the blaze
of your pink dress

Glowing against
the oncoming obsidian night

Forty-Six

I remember Lew Welch's line
about Muses and Mistresses

About confusion
about trouble

And I thought I knew
what he meant

Until the wind
from her hair

Blew both my way

The Mizpah Sonnet

She stands naked at the window
skin glowing from the bath pulls
the lace curtain over to one side

Pink rain pulsed motel neon
reflecting up from five floors
below dapples her alabaster profile

In gray light she will reach
for him soon she'll come
across the bed to his warmth

And with the breast of Redlick Summit
draped in dark nimbus rain turning
to snow they'll head north then west

Through the world's longest deepest valley
peaks on either side stiff with late spring snow

Red Mountain

In the Mojave amidst
miles of solar collectors
a forest of windmills

She sits legs crossed leaning
back against the beer cooler
her cutoffs barely coming

To the top of her thigh oh
so white against the black
naugahyde with one hand

She lifts her hair from
the back of her neck holds
it on top of her head

A sinuous mass of red vipers
below which one black mule
dangles from red painted toes

The other mule hooks
the rung of the stool moves
to Chet's elegiac trumpet as

She reaches back into
the cooler for a piece of ice
presses it against her neck

The melt runs down to
faux white pearl snaps
on her tight black top

Straining to contain what comes to
mind she says *well up till now been
nothin' but heat and wind round here*

Desert Saudade

What seems to matter most
is how it matters still

How the wind can become
the achingly beautiful recognition
of a sad song's yearning

An end of the world waltz
through the slate black
Great Basin night where
absence becomes presence

Where we turned
lost temporarily
what it was
we thought we had

Blinker suddenly on
right lane
turning left
to nowhere

Ninety miles out

And wondering why

Just

Past

Labor

Day

Rodeo's in Town

The gaggle of tanned cowgirl poptarts
a stunning array of the tightest Wranglers
every conceivable color you can imagine
wiggling their asses and cooing to one
another as they bend over the mirrors
at the cosmetic counter in Raley's

Heart's Correlative

Each and every moment of pain balanced by
an equal and opposite moment of pleasure

Local Knowledge

Wyatt around

Nope

When's he comin'

Dunno

You're just
a fuckin' fountain
of information

Ain't you

Don't matter
what I say

It'll turn out
to be wrong

Erotic

The knowledge
the conviction

That you are wanted

From there
it's but a short step

To going too far enough

Fulcrum

Sure we can think
about it that way
if you like

We can perhaps
talk about what
it all means

Try to define
what we believe
what we want

Wonder what or who
is God what or who
will make us happy

Ponder the differences
between involvement
and commitment

Watch those definitions
change transmute into
first one thing then

Another wind whipped
clouds or a sudden burst
of sparrows from the lilacs

But now let's simply applaud
the sight of you wiggling
out of your jeans unhinging

Your bra turning toward
me with the smile that
makes us both realize

The best thing about today
is that it could just become
tomorrow again and again

Finding at last balancing
a promise with what lasts

Nevada Weather

If you don't like it
you can either

Wait fifteen minutes

Or

Look out another
window of the house

Scenes from the French Revolution

How just exactly at sunset the two peacocks
fly up top of the telephone pole perch there

As if to get one last glimpse of the dying light
briefly the blaze of their iridescent blue breasts

Backlit by the rising silver dollar moon
almost makes you forget how earlier

They were just two more marauding peasants
busily intent on ransacking your garden

Amor Fati

Always late never early
she thinks she's both

Worth every painful moment
worth less for causing it

Can see Tuesday
turn to Wednesday

Without regret and
wants you to forget

She gives you reason
again and again not to

Night Music

You don't notice at first
how it starts slowly from
far off the single plop
plop of drops

On the last of fall's leaves
a slightly off-key sonata

Moving from cottonwood
to fledgling cherry
over Russian olive
to where it must really end

Suddenly it is so quiet
you forget how it began
listen again and again
for the first telltale notes

Her moving toward you like
small arpeggios from the west

Yes it's late but maybe never too
you tell yourself her touch will
come when it does when she
rests in your arms once again

Even the rain when it falls
will feel like it's coming home

Morna

Somewhere out there this month's rosy cheeked
pomegranate incarnation of the moon rises above
the night's excessively inflated bouffant petticoats

Combs the snarls from her hair and remembering
that time years ago far to the west of here how he
carried her how she pulled him toward her light

Gave her pause for a moment just for a moment
it all came rushing swirling back and so she felt
around under the Stillwaters for this morning's

Hastily kicked off shiny patent pumps slipped into them
and slowly began to climb the sad tattered obsidian stairs

Lure

Just what is it
what thing so
hooks my eye

The neon backlit
swollen web of
her amber hair

The rhythm
her heels beat
on the sidewalk

Or is it a glimpse
just the glimpse
briefly through

The slit skirt
the tops of her
black stockings

That snags my
mind pulls it
toward a sense

Other than common
filled with thoughts
of just what might be

Cellaring

He once thought of her as the wine
you put away when company comes
hints of a great body nicely finished

Even now in the musty breath of late
autumn what there was left remained
distinct a blood red vintage of its own

Which he drank to her memory

Or not

Poetry Readings, Dim Bulbs &
Bad Renditions of Chamber Music

Although it has been said that
you can get through anything
if you know it's going to end

Sometimes in the midst of it all
it begins to seem that it will
never change never end never

The longer it lasts the longer
they drone on and on and on

The less you seem to care

Just Past Labor Day

Sleep will become
a language spoken

Only in a distant
country where the air

Stills suddenly chills
the penumbral hours

Before dawn memories
of August's passionate

Heat recede while
the silent evasive

Demon of doubt
begins to show you

How water can enter stone
fracture the heart of the matter

Acknowledgments

The author would like to thank the editors/publishers of the following magazines and anthologies where some of these poems first appeared, sometimes in different form:

A, Abraxas, American Freeway: Best of American Small Press Poets (Maro Verlag), The American Literary Review, American Poets Say Goodbye to the Twentieth Century (Four Walls, Eight Windows), The Americas Anthology (New Rivers Press), Amorotica: New Erotic Poetry (Deep River), Arts Alive, Benzene, Blackjack, Cafe Solo, Cenizas: Literature & Art, Cloudline, Cold Drill, The Coldsprings Journal, Contemporary Quarterly, Correspondence Art (Visual Arts Press), Coyote's Journal, Crawlspace, Desert Wood: An Anthology of Nevada Poets (University of Nevada Press), The Echo, Et Cetera, Fireweed, Five Card Stud: Five Contemporary Poets (Duck Down), Floating Island, Gasolin, A Geography of Poets (Bantam), The Greenfield Review, High Country News, Home Planet News, Hyperion, Idaho Arts Journal, In Focus, Intermedia, Interstate, Invisible City, Italia America, Kaldron, Kangaroo Court, Kudzu, The Lahontan Valley News, The Limberlost Review, A Long Line of Joy (Big Boulevard), Madrona, The McLean County Poetry Review, The Meadows, Men Talk (Deep River), Mojo Navigator(e), neon, Nevada Magazine, The Nevada Weekly, New Directions, A New Geography of Poets (University of Arkansas Press), New Work(s) (Duck Down), Nexus, O.Ars, Offerta Speciale, Olympia, On the Bus, Open Ring, The Orchard, Oro Madre, Orpheus, The Pikestaff Forum, PinchPenny, Poetry NOW, Poetry of the American Indian (American Visual Communications), Purr, Reno Gazette-Journal, road/house, Rocky Mountain Creative Arts Journal, Scree, Seven Nevada Poets (Black Rock Press), 616 Center 1, The Smudge, Snowy Egret, South Dakota Review, The Stoogism Anthology (Scarecrow), Street, Swamp Root, Sweet Little Sixteen, Telephone, Terpentin on the Rocks: Poems from the Small Presses of the U.S. (Maro Verlag), Thorn Apple, TumbleWords: Writers Reading the West (University of Nevada Press), Uzzano, Vagabond, The Vagabond Anthology, Wanbli Ho, West Conscious Review, Whetstone, Wind, Wine Rings, The Wormwood Review, and Yellow Brick Road.

Two of the poems also appeared as broadsides from the Black Rock Press.

Books/Chapbooks by Kirk Robertson

The Burning Fire Chief (1975)

Shooting at Shadows, Killing Crows (1975)

Drinking Beer at 22 Below (1976)

Walked on by 40 Camels (1977)

Sultry Afternoon with the Blinds Partly Pulled (1978)

Shovel Off to Buffalo (1978)

Under the Weight of the Sky (1978)

Coffee, Dust Devils & Old Rodeo Bulls (1979)

No Deposit, No Return (1980)

Nevada (1980)

Origins, Initiations (1980)

Reasons and Methods (1981)

West Nevada Waltz (1981)

Two Weeks Off (1977, 1984)

Art·i·facts (1985)

Matters of Equal Height (1987)

Driving to Vegas: New & Selected Poems, 1969–87 (1989)

Music: A Suite & 13 Songs (1995)